Finance for nonfinancial managers

Neil Seitz
Saint Louis University
St. Louis, Missouri

Reston Publishing Company, Inc.
A Prentice-Hall Company
Reston, Virginia

Library of Congress Cataloging in Publication Data

Seitz, Neil
Finance for nonfinancial managers.

Includes bibliographical references and index.
1. Business enterprises—Finance. 2. Corporations—Finance. I. Title.
HG4026.S385 1983 658.1'5 82-23006
ISBN 0-8359-1997-8
ISBN 0-8359-1996-X (pbk.)

Editorial supervision and
interior design by
Ginger Sasser DeLacey.
Cover design by
Carol Conway.

10 9 8 7 6 5 4 3 2 1

Printed in the United States of America

Contents

Preface

This book is for managers who recognize the importance of understanding the financial considerations affecting business decisions. High, unstable interest rates, a record number of business failures, and the increased influence of the company's financial executives have made many managers increasingly aware of the importance of finance, and of the personal benefits to be derived from an understanding of finance. They have sought additional knowledge about finance in record numbers, and this book is designed to meet their needs.

No background in accounting or finance is required to benefit from this book. For readers who are unaccustomed to reading financial reports, Chapter 2 will serve as a useful introduction to financial data. Chapters 3–5 cover the effective use of company financial data in more detail. Chapters 6–9 deal with the effective use of the company's resources, particularly money resources. The final two chapters deal with considerations involved in acquiring money from lenders and investors. This book covers both the tools of financial decision making and the major financial considerations involved in business decisions.

In writing this book, I accumulated many debts. Ted Buchholz at Reston Publishing Company brought the need for this book to my attention. Cheryl Seitz went beyond routine copyediting to improve consistency, clarity, and accuracy. Ginger DeLacey moved the book through production promptly and (almost) painlessly. Last, but not least, Bente, Laura, and Kirsten provided the understanding that made writing this book a pleasure.

To my parents
Everett and Anna Mae Seitz

1 Introduction

Managers in all areas of the organization have found that they must understand finance if they are to manage effectively. One factor that has led to the increased importance of finance is the rapid rise in the cost of money. In the 1950s, the interest rate on bank loans to good business customers moved in the range from 2 to 4 percent; the cost of money tied up in an ill-advised investment was not so painful. With bank lending rates now moving in the range from 10 percent to over 20 percent, the profitable use of all money has become imperative.

Another factor that has made finance important is instability. Prior to the 1970s, the interest rate banks charged to their best customers changed about 16 times each decade. In the year 1981 alone, the rate changed 25 times. The supply of funds as well as the cost was relatively assured in many past years. If a company with a good credit rating suddenly faced an unexpected need for money, it could be reasonably confident of both availability and cost. Today, companies are frequently told that due to another "credit crunch" it will be necessary for them to reduce their use of borrowing rather than increase it. Instability of interest rates and of supply have changed the rules under which all managers operate.

Though businesses must face increasingly complex financial problems, this is not a book of gloom. Success has always been achieved by businesses which deal with problems more effectively than do their competitors. Effective managers are dealing with the changing financial environment by recognizing the importance of financial realities and by integrating them into decisions at all levels. This book was written to help nonfinancial managers deal with the financial realities affecting their areas of responsibility and with the financial consequences of their decisions.

Financial marketplace

Although the focus of this book is on decision making within the individual business, it must be remembered that the business does not operate in isolation. In fact, it is the recognition of the impacts of changes in the general economy that has led to the increased attention given to finance. Because of the importance of changes in the financial environment outside the firm, it is useful to begin with a brief, wide-angle look at finance.

In its broadest sense, finance deals with any transactions in which money is exchanged for money rather than for goods or services. Most financial transactions involve the payment of money today with the expectation of receiving a greater amount in the future. These transactions involve stock and bond sales as well as bank loans. They also include capital investments within the firm, wherein an asset is purchased today with the expectation that it will provide cash flows in the future.

The market for money to use in making investments is quite similar to the markets for other goods, except for the matter of time. People who have saved money and do not wish to spend it for goods or services at the moment will seek the most profitable use for their money. They are the sellers (or lenders to be more accurate, since they expect to receive back their own money plus some additional money as rent). Households are the primary savers, though many of them invest their savings through financial institutions rather than personally searching for profitable uses.

The buyers in this marketplace are people or organizations who have some present use for funds and are willing to pay a rent to have funds available now. The primary users of funds are businesses, governments, and households. Typically, young households are net users of other people's funds while older households are net providers of funds to the financial markets.

The price in the financial markets—the rent for money—is determined in the same way as the price of any other product. If there is a shortage of money to borrow, the interest rate will be bid up until some potential users decide the price is too high and that they would rather forgo the intended investment or expenditure. If there are excess funds available, the interest rate will fall until additional people find the price attractive.

This bidding process does not occur in a single market location. The interest rates on stocks and bonds are bid up and down on the security exchanges. Interest rates on bank loans rise and fall as banks respond to changes in the volume of loan requests and savings deposits. Savers and users of funds interact in these and dozens of other markets to determine the interest rates at which supply and demand come into balance.

However, this market for money does not operate without outside interference. The government, through the central bank (Federal Reserve Bank in the United States), frequently acts to increase or decrease the supply of money available for borrowing.

The interest rate, or price of money, has shown increasing instability in recent years. This instability reflects a rapidly changing supply and demand situation caused by changing economic conditions, inflation, and actions by the government to increase or decrease the amount of money available for lending.

No business is immune to these swings in interest rates. A business in need of money to expand must raise those funds in the financial markets. Higher interest rates mean that assets must earn a higher return if the company is to meet the current cost of funds. Even the company that does not have an immediate need for new funds is affected by conditions in the financial markets. Management is expected to earn a return for the shareholders that is greater than or equal to what those shareholders can earn in alternative investments of equal risk. A rising interest rate means that returns on these alternative investments, too, are rising.

The pricing of money in the financial markets and the responses of companies to changing prices serve an important social function. Because money is a claim on goods and services, it is necessarily scarce. The interest rate provides a method of allocating this scarce resource. Since money will be acquired in the financial markets only if its use justifies the cost, it is allocated to the most efficient uses. Thus, companies responding to financial market conditions play an important part in the efficient allocation of resources. This efficient allocation results in increased wealth for the nation.

Objectives of financial management

Efficiency is the key word in understanding the objectives of financial management. The firm is under continual pressure to use financial resources as efficiently as possible if it is to realize its goals: to meet interest payments on debt, to earn a satisfactory return for owners, and to grow.

Although not as tangible as the pressure to meet interest on debt, the pressure to earn a return on the owner's funds is substantial and of prime concern to the corporation. If a company is to expand, it frequently faces the need to raise additional money from owners by selling additional stock. The ability to raise money in this way depends on the earning of a satisfactory return on funds already committed. Investors will refuse to commit additional funds to a company that is not earning a return on existing funds at least equal to what can be earned on other investments of the same risk.

Even if a company does not need to raise new funds, the well-being of the firm and that of its managers is strongly affected by the efficiency with which funds are used. Stock options and profit sharing plans are the most direct way managers benefit from efficient funds use. The price of the company's stock increases and decreases according to the investors' estimates of the profitability of the company's investments. Thus the value of the management compensation packages depends on the value of the company's stock and in turn on the efficient use of funds. The efficiency of funds use applies to the firms' investment in plant, equipment, and accounts receivable; it also applies to expenditures such as salaries and advertising campaigns.

Unfriendly takeovers are one of the pressures that have caused managers to focus sharply on financial performance. If a company's stock price is depressed because the company is not earning a satisfactory return on owners' funds, the company is a prime candidate for acquisition by some other corporation. The acquiring company can buy the stock at the depressed price, take control, and replace the present managers with people who will concentrate on managing more effectively and efficiently.

Even organizations without stockholders (e.g., savings and loan companies, hospitals and universities), are subject to most of the same pressures to use resources efficiently. They have specific objectives and limited financial resources with which to achieve them. They frequently borrow money, thereby competing directly in the financial markets. In addition, many nonprofit organizations seek charitable donations. To be successful in seeking such money, it is imperative that such organizations demonstrate efficient use of existing resources.

It is clear that all companies are under pressure to use their resources as efficiently as possible. Earning a profit is not enough; performance is measured in terms of profit earned per dollar of funds committed. The term *profitability* is frequently used to designate return measured in relation to funds invested and to differentiate between this return and simple profit. Profitability is judged in comparison to returns available through alternate investments available in the financial markets. This is the financial reality that every manager faces every business day.

Financial functions of the firm

Just as the financial manager should be aware of what goes on in manufacturing and the manufacturing manager should be aware of problems faced in marketing, every manager should be aware of the problems and functions of the financial manager. It is commonly said that the financial problems of the firm include raising funds in the financial markets, allocating those funds to their optimal uses within the firm, and following up to see that efficiency of usage is maintained. The following functions are carried out by the financial manager in helping the firm deal with these problems.

Planning. The financial manager frequently acts as the coordinator for both short- and long-range planning. The first facet of this function is budgeting: both operating budgets and budgets for capital expenditures. The second facet of the planning responsibility is the evaluation of performance against budgets and the analysis of acquisitions and divestitures.

Provision of funds. The financial manager is responsible for securing money needed by the firm which includes both short-term funds such as short-term bank loans and long-term funds such as bond issues and common stock issues. The financial manager is also responsible for planning for funds generated within the firm; for example, he recommends a dividend policy to the board of directors.

Administration of funds. Administration of funds involves the actual management of the firm's cash. The financial manager must develop proper control of receipt and disbursement and must maintain banking relationships. He must also oversee pension funds as well as other security investments of the firm. Credit policy is frequently controlled by the financial manager as part of the responsibility for administration of funds.

Protection of assets. The financial manager can see that the protection of assets is achieved through the development of sound insurance programs and proper internal controls, followed by internal auditing.

Tax administration. The financial manager is responsible for both the filing of tax reports with the government and for planning to minimize tax expense.

Investor relations. The company will find it much easier to raise funds if it maintains good relations with investors and potential investors on a regular basis. The financial manager maintains relations by communicating with stockholders and by keeping in contact with members of the investment community. The financial manager is responsible for arranging meetings with the security analysts who prepare recommendations about the stocks and bonds of particular companies. The financial manager also maintains relations with the investment bankers who help the company sell new issues of stocks and bonds.

Management information systems. The financial manager is frequently responsible for the management of the company's electronic data processing facilities. He may also be responsible for design of the information systems used in connection with those facilities.

Organization of the finance function

The organization of the finance function in a typical large firm is summarized in Figure 1-1. The vice-president for finance answers directly to the president and interacts with the finance committee of the board of directors, which makes recommendations to the board concerning matters such as dividend policy, choice of financing methods, and acquisition of other companies. Under the vice-president for finance are the controller and treasurer. The controller is responsible for the accounting function while the treasurer is responsible for the provision and administration of funds. Although some duties may be assigned to the controller in one company and to

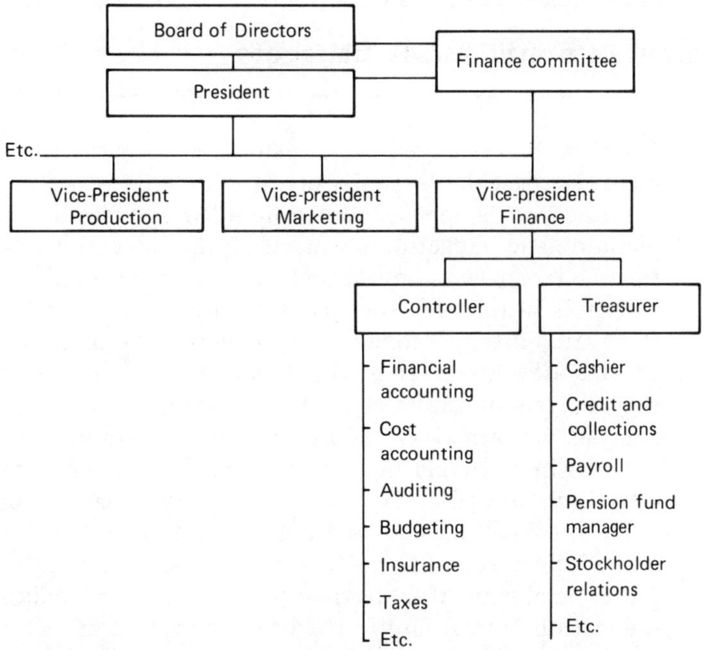

Figure 1–1 Financial organization of the firm

the treasurer in another, the division of duties reflects their primary responsibilities. In connection with the accounting function, the controller usually has responsibility for preparing reports on the financial performance of the business (financial accounting), developing ways to measure cost through cost accounting, performing audits, budgeting, and sometimes for managing the company's insurance program and taxes. The treasurer manages the actual cash of the business as well as managing payroll and credits and collections. The treasurer is responsible for the management of the firm's pension funds as well. In addition, the treasurer has responsibility for maintaining relationships with stockholders, banks, and other present or potential sources of funds. The treasurer is also involved in the budgeting and planning process as part of planning for money needs and may have responsibility for insurance and taxes.

The structure in Figure 1–1 describes a large company. It becomes greatly streamlined when a small corporation is involved. There may be a single person who is responsible for all the functions of the financial manager, even in a company so big that all of these functions must be performed.

Involvement of nonfinancial managers

One who has observed the decision making activities of firms will recognize that the financial manager frequently serves a coordinating function, as opposed to having sole responsibility. For example, planning and budgeting are carried out at all levels of the firm; the financial manager's unique responsibility is in coordinating all these activities in terms of their combined impact on profitability, risk, the availability of money, etc. Likewise, the profitability analysis carried out or overseen by the financial manager in connection with the analysis of capital investment proposals is only one type of analysis performed on such proposals; its importance is as a coordinating input in relating the project to the firm's profitability goals. Certainly, the chief executive officer and board of directors will make the final decision with regard to how money is to be raised when it is needed. The financial manager's responsibility encompasses analyzing the alternatives available and making a recommendation with regard to the best alternative in light of economic conditions and company needs.

There have been a number of cases of firms getting into difficulty through poor financial management (poor budgeting controls, poor planning for funds needs, etc.), but the financial manager cannot turn unprofitable decisions into profitable ones by financial manipulations. Only effective management at all levels within the company can achieve the profitability objective. It is for this reason that managers at all levels must be constantly aware of the financial environment in which they operate and of the impacts of their decisions on the financial position of the firm.

There is an increasing awareness of the importance of finance to managers at all levels within the firm. As a result, there have been numerous efforts, including this book, to increase understanding of the financial aspects of decision making. Those who master the material in this book will gain useful tools with which to understand financial considerations and to increase their effectiveness as managers.

2

Understanding financial statements

The financial statements of a company not only give a picture of its current status but also of the things that have happened in its past. A person who is familiar with these statements can learn much about the company's past actions as well as the courses of action that will improve its performance in the future. Therefore, financial statements are used by managers at all levels as well as by lenders, investors, and any other outsiders interested in the company's performance, and it is for this reason that accounting is frequently referred to as the language of business.

The financial statements can be divided into two broad categories: external and internal. The external financial statements are prepared for use by people outside the company, such as lenders and stockholders. They serve to report what management has done with the resources supplied to the company; the term *stewardship accounting* is frequently used with regard to these financial statements. The primary external reports are the *income statement,* with it associated statement of retained earnings, and the *balance sheet.* The source and use of funds statement serves to supplement these two primary statements.

The accuracy of the external financial reports must be verified by a certified public accountant who serves as an independent professional rather than as an employee of the firm. The certified public accountant must verify that the information presented to the public is accurate and that the company's actions are recorded in accordance with generally accepted accounting principles established by the *Financial Accounting Standards Board,* a national board given the responsibility for developing financial reporting guidelines. The maintenance of common guidelines provides at least some basis for comparison between companies and over time.

Internal accounting, also referred to as *management accounting,* deals with the preparation of accounting reports for the use of managers in making decisions. A major part of managerial accounting work consists of *cost accounting:* determining the costs of a particular action so the company can then determine whether that action is profitable. A cost accounting system that accurately measures the cost of producing each product is a major aid in setting price and in determining which products to produce. Budgeting and planning are also parts of management accounting. In addition, companies sometimes prepare income statements and balance sheets for internal use that are different from those prepared for external use because they do not feel the form required for external use provides them the most useful information possible.

Income statement

The income statement is designed to describe what has happened to the company over a certain period of time. Specifically, it shows the company's income and expenses over that time period. This information is needed to determine if the company has been profitable in the past and to develop plans for achieving profitability in the future.

In order to interpret the information in the income statement, one should be familiar with some of the problems the accountant faces when preparing a financial statement. With regard to the income statement, one of the most difficult problems is determining when income and expenses occurred. This might seem like a trivial problem until one considers the inventory that a company purchased on credit in 1980, paid for in 1981, sold on credit in 1982, and received payment for in 1983. In preparing a single income statement for the four-year period, the sale price would be recognized as income and the purchase price would be recognized as expense. However, an income statement would be needed for each year. Was an expense incurred when the inventory was purchased in 1980, when it was paid for in 1981, or when it was sold? Was it sold when it was delivered to the customer in 1982 or when the payment was received in 1983? To analyze an income statement, one must understand how accountants have solved these problems.

One approach to the question of when to recognize income or expense is the cash method of accounting which is recognizing income or expense when cash flows in or out. Because this method has the advantage of being very simple, it is used by small businesses. But, it can result in serious distortion of income. Suppose, for example, a company purchases inventory for cash in one period and sells it for cash in the next. Using the cash method, a loss would be reported in the period inventory was purchased and a large profit would be reported for the period of sale; the income statements would give an inaccurate picture of the company's profits for both periods.

Most companies rely on the *accrual method* of accounting, recognizing income and expenses when they occur, not when cash is paid or received. For example, a sale is generally recognized at the time title to the item sold passes to the new owner, not the time of the agreement to sell or the time of payment of the bill. The accrual method also recognizes that the acquisition of an asset for use in a later period is an expense in the period it is used, not the period in which it was acquired or paid for.

The income statement of Inboard Motor Corporation, a medium-sized manufacturer, appears in Table 2–1. It will be referred to in the following paragraphs which explain the meaning of the various components of the income statement in light of the accrual method of accounting.

Net sales. Inboard Motor Corporation recognizes sales according to the standard approach of passage of title. As a practical matter, this normally means that a sale occurs in the period in which the product is delivered to the customer or turned over to a public freight carrier for shipment to the customer. Thus, sales represent items actually delivered or shipped to customers in 1982. The term "net sales" is used because allowances are made for returns and for bad debts from credit customers. "Net sales" is the amount the company has received or expects to receive after allowing for these problems.

Cost of goods sold. If a dealer buys a motor from Inboard Motor and subsequently resells it, the dealer's cost of goods sold is quite easy to determine; it is the amount he has paid or has agreed to pay to

Table 2-1 Inboard Motor Company

Income statement
for the year ending December 31, 1982
(000 omitted on all but per share data)

Net sales	$687,398
Cost of goods sold	542,748
Gross profit	144,650
Operating expenses	
Selling and advertising	73,149
General and administrative	48,651
	121,800
Earnings from operations	22,850
Interest expense	20,358
Earnings before provision for income taxes	2,492
Provision for income taxes	148
Net earnings for the year	2,344
Net earnings per share of common stock	$.28

Statement of accumulated retained earnings	
Balance at beginning of year	$237,851
Add—net earnings	2,344
	240,195
Deduct—cash dividends	1,890
Balance at the end of the year	$238,305

Inboard for the motor. However, the problem is considerably more complex for a manufacturer like Inboard. Inboard built a factory, bought materials, and hired workers in order to build the motor. Somehow, the company must determine what portion of those costs are associated with this particular motor.

Under accrual accounting, the accountant recognizes the cost of manufacturing an item by reporting that the company owns inventory with a value equal to the cost of manufacturing it. When the item is subsequently sold, the sale price is recognized as revenue and the value (cost) is recognized as an expense. This is referred to as the matching approach because the accountant attempts to match the time of expense recognition with the time of sales recognition.

In a complex business world, there are always difficult questions about which costs are associated with which product. Some costs are referred to as direct costs because they can be easily associated with a particular product. These would include such things as raw materials used and labor spent directly on that product. However, there are also expenses that occur in production, but that are not easily assigned to a particular product. For example, the factory may have a limited life of twenty years. The accountant will report an expense each year equal to some portion of the original cost of the factory to recognize this wearing out as an expense. Other such expenses are factory maintenance, electricity costs, and insurance on the factory. Although these indirect costs are difficult to associate with any particular unit produced, the accountant must develop an assignment method, even if it is somewhat arbitrary. These costs are originally allocated to the items produced and shown in the balance sheet portion of the company's records as part of the value of inventory held by the company. They are recognized as expenses only when the product is sold or otherwise disposed of.

Depreciation represents a particularly difficult cost problem. Before attempting to assign depreciation expenses to the value of a product, the accountant must determine the amount of the depreciation expense for a particular year. To do this it is necessary to estimate the useful life and salvage value of the factory or piece of equipment to be depreciated, then choose a depreciation method. The simplest method is *straight-line* depreciation. The difference between original cost and final value is simply divided by the number of years of useful life to determine the annual depreciation. For example, a piece of equipment that costs \$200,000, has a ten-year expected life and no value at the end of its useful life, will have annual straight-line depreciation of:

$$\text{straight-line depreciation} = \$200{,}000/10 = \$20{,}000$$

The depreciation amount will be the same during each year of the equipment's life.

As an alternative to straight-line depreciation, an accelerated depreciation method may be chosen if the asset is expected to lose value in its earlier years faster than in later years. This type of assumption is frequently reasonable. A new car with an expected life of ten years might lose 20 percent of its value in the first year. An example of a widely used accelerated depreciation method is the *double-declining-balance method.* With the double-declining-balance method, the percent of the asset's value recognized as depreciation each year is twice that of the straight-line method, but the percentage is applied to the asset's value at the beginning of the year rather than to its original cost. For the asset used as an example of straight-line depreciation, the first-year double-declining-balance (DDB) depreciation would be:

$$\text{first-year DDB depreciation} = 0.20 \times \$200{,}000 = \$40{,}000$$

At the beginning of the second year, the value of the asset has therefore been reduced to $160,000 ($200,000 − $40,000). Depreciation for the second year is then:

$$\text{second-year DDB depreciation} = 0.20 \times \$160{,}000 = \$32{,}000$$

Total depreciation will be the same over the life of the asset under each method. However, depreciation in a particular year can vary considerably according to which method is chosen. This affects the value assigned to items produced and therefore can affect reported income when those items are sold. When comparing companies, it is important to check the footnotes to the financial statements and determine if they are using the same depreciation methods.

Even after the value of each item added to inventory has been determined, the accountant still faces the problem of determining which item to recognize as sold. The two most widely used approaches are last-in, first-out (LIFO) and first-in, first-out (FIFO).

Consider a company that produced two units of a particular product for inventory. It cost $100 to produce the first unit, but rising prices of raw materials led to a $200 cost for the second unit. A total inventory value of $300 was then reported on the balance sheet. Following this, the company sold one unit. Using the last-in, first-out (LIFO) method, the cost of goods sold would be $200 and the remaining inventory value would be $100. Using the first-in, first-out (FIFO) method, the cost of goods sold would be $100 and the remaining inventory value would be $200.

Gross profit is, of course, simply the difference between net sales and the cost of goods sold.

Operating expenses are expenses for the year that are not associated with the production of a specific product. They include administrative expenses such as salaries associated with the management of the company as well as the expenses associated with marketing the firm's products.

Earnings from operations equal gross earnings minus operating expenses. It is a particularly useful number because it represents income before paying a return on money invested in the firm; it separates the results of operating decisions from the effects of decisions as to how to raise money from investors. For this reason, it is frequently referred to as *net operating income.*

Interest expense represents the first element of the cost of funds provided to the firm by investors. Interest is, of course, the rent on money borrowed. Following the accrual approach, the interest expense item represents interest that accrued during the year, whether or not it was paid. Suppose, for example, that Inboard owed interest for December 1982, but was late in paying it and did not actually make the payment until January 1983. The interest would still be recognized as an expense of 1982, not the year in which the obligation was actually paid.

Earnings before provision for income taxes simply represent income after all expenses except income taxes.

Provision for income taxes, like other expense items, represents expenses incurred during the year, whether or not they were actually paid. At the close of 1982, the company determined its income tax liability for the year. The company had made quarterly payments based on estimated income and may have paid more or less than the amount owed for the year (normally less). Even if part of the tax was paid in 1983 or later, it is recognized as an expense of the year in which the liability was created.

Net earnings for the year is the amount left after taxes are deducted from earnings before taxes. A point important enough to deserve reiteration is that income is *not* cash flow. Sales may or may not have resulted in cash payments, expenses may or may not have been paid in cash, and assets that were purchased do not show up as expense items on the income statement except as they are being worn out.

Net earnings per share of common stock. All corporations issue common stock. This represents the ownership position; investors who make their investment by purchasing the company's common stock are the ultimate owners. Residual earnings after all other claims have been paid are owned collectively by the common stockholders. The members of the board of directors, elected by the common shareholders to oversee the company and manage their investment, determine how much of the earnings should be reinvested and how much should be returned to the common stockholders.

In addition to the sale of common stock, some companies raise money by selling preferred stock. Preferred stock usually receives a fixed dividend payment each year and does not participate in earnings beyond that. (Other provisions related to preferred stock are covered in Chapter 10.) The remaining earnings accrue to the benefit of the common stockholders, whether paid out to them or reinvested to earn even greater earnings. The net earnings per share of common stock represent the net earnings remaining after paying preferred dividends, divided by the average number of shares of common stock outstanding during the year.

Statement of consolidated retained earnings

Immediately following the income statement is the statement of accumulated retained earnings. As the statement indicates, the company had accumulated retained earnings of $237,851 thousand at the end of 1981. To this amount was added the 1982 net income of $2,344 thousand. From that total, $1,890 thousand of dividends paid were subtracted to give accumulated retained earnings of $238,305 thousand at the end of 1982.

The most important thing to know about accumulated retained earnings is what it is not: it is *not* cash that the company has available to spend. Accumulated retained earnings is simply the difference between total income since the company was formed and total dividends over that same time period. Since income was not necessarily cash, there is no reason to believe that the difference between income and dividends would be cash. If we want to know how much cash a company has available to invest, we must turn to the balance sheet and look at the account labeled "cash."

Balance sheet

The balance sheet is a snapshot of the financial position of the firm at a particular instant as opposed to the income statement which reports activities over a certain time period. The balance sheets in Table 2-2 are snapshots of Inboard Motor Corporation's financial structure at midnight on December 31, 1981 and 1982.

The balance sheet is divided into two parts. The first part reports the value of the assets owned by the corporation while the second part—liabilities and stockholders' equity—reports the amount owed by the firm and the value of the owners' investment. Since it is a matter of definition that the value of the owners' investment is the difference between what the company owns and what it owes, the sum of the second part of the balance sheet always equals the sum of the asset part. This relationship is commonly referred to as the basic accounting equation:

total assets = total liabilities + owners' investment

Table 2-2 Inboard Motor Corporation

Balance sheets for December 31, 1981 and 1982
(000 omitted)

Assets	*1982*	*1981*
Current assets:		
Cash and time deposits	$ 34,454	$ 15,853
Accounts receivable	122,364	118,618
less allowance for doubtful accounts	900	804
	121,464	117,814
Inventories	194,122	221,668
Prepaid expenses	22,534	21,589
Total current assets	372,574	376,924
Plant and equipment	332,006	330,251
less accumulated depreciation	162,387	147,433
	169,619	182,818
Total assets	$542,193	$559,742
Liabilities and stockholders' investment	*1982*	*1981*
Current liabilities		
Accounts payable	$ 36,086	$ 41,657
Accrued liabilities	46,391	46,764
Accrued taxes	8,732	9,425
Notes payable	19,000	25,396
Current maturities of long-term debt	2,869	1,951
Total current liabilities	113,078	125,193
Long-term debt	112,772	123,685
Deferred pension plan contributions	2,071	1,316
Total liabilities	227,921	250,194
Stockholders' investment		
Preferred stock—$10 par	37,050	32,780
Common stock	2,506	2,506
Capital in excess of par value of common stock	36,411	36,411
Accumulated retained earnings	238,305	237,851
	314,272	309,548
Total liabilities and equity	$542,193	$559,742

Both parts of the balance sheet can be divided between current and long-term items. Current assets are cash and items that are expected to be used up or converted to cash within one year. Current liabilities are obligations of the company that are due within one year. The term *working capital* is used in discussing these current assets and liabilities. Total working capital is synonymous with total current assets, and net working capital equals current assets minus current liabilities.

Each of the balance sheet accounts is examined in the following paragraphs.

Cash and time deposits. The cash balance shown on a balance sheet includes both the currency held by the company and the balances in its checking accounts. In this case, time deposit balances were included in this one account because the company freely moves funds between time deposits and checking accounts on a daily basis to make the most efficient use possible of temporarily idle funds.

Accounts receivable. The first number ($122,364 thousand) represents the amount actually owed to Inboard Motor by its customers. However, the company recognizes that some customers will default on their payments. When a sale occurs, a small amount is deducted from the sale to represent the proportion of accounts that are expected to default. The net sale figure on the income statement represents total sales minus these expected losses. The sale is recorded in the accounts receivable portion of the balance sheet by adding the sale amount to accounts receivable and by adding the allowance for defaults to the reserve for doubtful accounts. When a particular customer's account is deemed uncollectable, that amount is subtracted from both the accounts receivable and the allowance for doubtful accounts, leaving the net figure unchanged.

Inventory. As was pointed out earlier, when an item is purchased or produced, its cost is originally added to inventory. When a sale occurs, the cost of goods sold is subtracted from sales to yield gross income. The cost of goods sold is also subtracted from the value of inventory on the balance sheet. The previously discussed problems involved in determining the cost of goods sold also affect the value of inventory reported on the balance sheet.

Prepaid income taxes. A prepaid tax occurs when the company pays tax on income that will be recognized in a later period rather than this period. This might occur because the taxing agency requires a different accounting method than that used to report to shareholders. In the case of Inboard Motor, the prepaid tax is a current asset indicating that it is tax paid on income to be recognized in 1983.

Other prepaid expenses. This account also represents items that were paid for this year, but that will be recognized as expenses next year. For example, if the company paid premiums for one year's insurance on July 1, 1982, half the payment would be treated as an expense of 1982 and the other half would be shown as a prepaid expense at the end of 1982. The amount carried as a prepaid expense would then be recognized as an expense on the 1983 income statement.

Plant and equipment. The plant and equipment account includes the value of land, buildings, machinery, automobiles, etc. In general, it includes any physical asset that is not held as the inventory for resale and has an expected useful life of more than one year, and is used in the operation of the business.[1] The first number ($332,006 thousand) is the cost of the company's plant and equipment.

As was pointed out in the discussion of the income statement, the company recognizes the fact that many of these assets wear out. The accumulated depreciation account represents the total decrease in value of all presently owned plant and equipment that has been recognized since those assets were acquired. The net amount of $169,619 thousand in 1982 is the total cost minus accumulated depreciation. On the company's internal records, there will be an account for each asset, showing its cost and its accumulated depreciation. When the asset is "fully depreciated," the accumulated depreciation equals the cost. If an asset is sold or disposed of, both its cost and its accumulated depreciation are removed from the plant and equipment account.

Accounts payable represent material or services that the firm has purchased, but has not yet paid for; one company's accounts payable are another company's accounts receivable. As current liabilities, they are to be paid in one year or less.

Accrued liabilities are expenses that have been recognized, but not yet paid for. These might include such things as the electricity that was used in December 1982, but that the company has not yet been billed for. The company will also have some accrued wages due at most times because workers earn their wages every day, but are only paid at certain weekly or monthly intervals.

Accrued taxes are taxes that are owed for 1982, but were not paid in 1982. For example, it is common practice to file a quarterly tax estimate fifteen days after the end of the quarter. This would mean that Inboard Motor's fourth-quarter estimated tax would not be paid until January 15, 1983. Therefore, it would be shown as an accrued tax on the December 31, 1982 balance sheet.

Notes payable represent money borrowed by Inboard Motor. This could be bank borrowing or borrowing from some other lender.

---

[1] If an asset were held for speculation rather than use, it would be reported as an *investment.*

Since the notes are shown as a current liability, they are due within one year.

It is worth stressing again that the asset part of the balance sheet shows where the money went and the liability and owner's equity part shows the composition of claims. The notes payable balance is no indication of the amount of money the company has. That amount is determined by looking at the cash item on the balance sheet.

Current maturities of long-term debt. Many company debt obligations are like the mortgage and automobile loans of individuals in that they call for repayment by a series of payments on some regular monthly or annual schedule. The payments on long-term debt that are due within the next year are carried as current maturities of long-term debt. The amount shown in this account is for principal payment (reduction in the amount owed) and does not include the scheduled interest payments, which are a rent on the money borrowed.

Long-term debt. As its name indicates, the long-term debt account reports money owed to lenders that is not scheduled for repayment in the next year. This may represent a bank loan with a longer maturity, a loan from a life insurance company, money borrowed by selling bonds to the public, or money borrowed from any other source. Bonds are frequently found selling below their face value (the amount the company has promised to repay at the due date) because interest rates have risen since the bond was issued. However, the value shown in the balance sheet is the value of the bonds when they were issued, not the current market value.

Deferred pension plan contribution. The liability side of the balance sheet will frequently have several categories of deferred items. Like the accrued liabilities in the current liability section, these represent amounts that the company is obliged to pay at some later date. The Employee Retirement Income Security Act of 1974 required that employees pay enough money into a separate fund to ensure that money would be available to make promised pension payments. The amount coming due from the employer each period is recognized as an expense on the income statement. The deferred pension plan contribution is the amount that has been recognized as an expense but not yet paid.

Stockholders' investment. The difference between what the company owns and what it owes is the stockholders' investment. It is broken down into categories according to how funds were raised from the stockholders.

Preferred stock. Many companies issue two kinds of stock, preferred and common. Preferred stock is frequently referred to as quasi-equity because it has some of the features of debt and some of the features of equity. Preferred stockholders normally receive a fixed dividend rather than participation in earnings, but the company's commitment to pay that dividend does not have the same legal status as the commitment to pay interest on debt. The details of the rights of preferred shareholders are discussed in Chapter 10. The par value of preferred stock is the amount that would be due to the holder if the company liquidated and there was anything left after paying the creditors. The total of the par values of all the preferred shares outstanding is $37,050 thousand.

The market value of a share of preferred stock may be entirely different from its par value. The market value is set by bids to buy and sell between investors. The market value is not only affected by returns available on alternate investments but also by changes in the company's standing as an investment risk.

Common stock. The remaining three accounts represent the common stockholders' investment. As the common stockholders are the ultimate owners of the firm, their investment includes both the amount they originally gave to the company in exchange for stock and earnings of the company that have not been paid out in dividends. The account listed as common stock represents the par value of a share of common stock multiplied by the total number of shares of common stock issued.

In most states, companies are required to list a par value for their stocks. Since there are sometimes taxes based on the par value, it is common practice to use a par value of $1; however, the company need not sell stock at this par value. For an existing company, the price at which additional stock is sold depends on the price at which existing stock is being bought and sold in the stock markets. For a new company, the price at which it sells its shares is somewhat arbitrary. The total dollars it raises from common stock represent total ownership. The price per share merely determines how many pieces of paper these owners will receive. A new company might, for example, establish a par value of $1 and sell its stock for $20 a share. The difference between par value and the price the stock is sold for is recorded as capital in excess of par value of common stock.

Capital in excess of par value of common stock. Suppose a company uses a common stock par value of $1 and sells new common stock for $20. The accountant will record the sale of one share by adding $1 to common stock and the remaining $19 to capital in excess of par value. Thus, this account is also referred to as contributed capital. The two accounts taken together are a measure of the amount of outside funds shareholders have invested in the company.

Accumulated retained earnings employed in the business. This account is more frequently referred to as simply retained earnings and represents the difference between total income and total dividends since the company was formed. It is an investment of the shareholders only to the extent that they could have invested their funds somewhere else if dividends had been equal to income.

The total of the preceding three accounts represents the total investment of the owners. This sum is commonly referred to as *owners' equity* or *net worth.* Sometimes mentioned is the book value of a share of common stock. The book value equals owners' equity divided by the number of shares of common stock outstanding. The market value, which may be substantially different than this book value, is determined through bids to buy and sell in the stock markets and is affected by expected profitability and dividends of the company compared to returns from alternative investments.

Statement of changes in financial position

The statement of changes in financial position is a report on causes of increase or decrease in the net working capital. It is necessary to supplement this report with only a look at increases and decreases in individual working capital accounts to develop a complete picture of the company's cash flows over the year. The statement of changes for Inboard Motor Corporation appears in Table 2–3.

Earnings from operations. This is simply the net income as reported on the income statement. Changes in net working capital will be determined by adding to and subtracting from this account.

Depreciation is added to income in developing a statement of cash flows because it was originally deducted from income as an expense though it involved no payment to anyone.

Deferred items. The increase in the deferred items accounts on the balance sheet (deferred pension contribution in this case) represents another expense that was deducted from income, but not paid for. Thus, it is also added back to income.

Proceeds from issue of preferred stock. In trying to look at cash flow rather than income, any source of cash inflow is significant. This company sold additional preferred stock for $4,270 thousand in

Table 2–3 Inboard Motor Corporation

Statement of changes in financial position, 1980
(000 omitted)

Sources of working capital	
Earnings from operations	$ 2,344
Charges against operations not requiring a current outlay of working capital	
Depreciation	14,954
Deferred items	755
	18,053
Proceeds from the issue of preferred stock	4,270
	22,323
Working capital used	
Additions to plant and equipment	1,755
Long-term debt paid or maturing currently	10,913
Dividends	1,890
	14,558
Increase in working capital	$ 7,765

1982. If it had issued additional long-term debt or common stock, that would be added as a source of net working capital as well.

Additions to plant and equipment is simply the amount of new plant and equipment purchased or constructed by the company during the year.

Long-term debt paid or maturing currently. The discussion of the balance sheet made mention that the portion of long-term debt that is due within one year is carried as a current liability. Since the statement of changes is a summary of the factors that led to increases or decreases in net working capital, the transfer of an amount from long-term debt to current maturities of long-term debt represents an increase in current liabilities and therefore a decrease in net working capital. If wanting to know how much long-term debt was actually repaid during the year, the total of long-term debt and current maturities for 1981 and 1982 can be compared. The difference between the two represent the net of long-term debt issued and repaid.

Dividends paid out were not deducted as an expense in computing income; therefore, they must be deducted from income in computing funds flow.

The above additions to and subtractions from net income summarize the factors that led to changes in the company's net working

Table 2–4 Inboard Motor Corporation

Analysis of changes in cash
year ending December 31, 1982
(000 omitted)

Sources of cash	
Increase in net working capital	$ 7,765
Decrease in inventory	27,546
Increase in current portion of long-term debt	918
	36,229
Uses of cash	
Increase in accounts receivable, net of allowance for doubtful accounts	3,650
Increase in prepaid expenses	945
Decrease in accounts payable	5,571
Decrease in accrued liabilities	373
Decrease in accrued taxes	693
Decrease in notes payable	6,396
	17,628
Increase in cash and time deposits	$18,601

capital. The changes in cash equal the change in net working capital plus increases in current liabilities, minus increases in non-cash current assets. This analysis is completed in Table 2–4.

Some cautions

Accounting statements carried out to the exact penny for a billion dollar corporation give the illusion of great accuracy. While these statements do provide extremely useful information, their accuracy should not be overestimated. As was illustrated earlier in this chapter, the level of profit and the value of assets can be significantly affected by the methods chosen to depreciate assets and value inventory. Methods used to compute pension fund liabilities and measure lease obligations also affect income and asset value. Thus, it is important to keep in mind that accounting statements are the income and value estimates of someone else.

And because the financial statements are someone's estimate of value and income, it is important to know who made the estimate. Audited financial statements have been verified by an independent certified public accountant. The certified public accountant has checked to be sure the company has used generally accepted accounting principles in reporting income. In addition, the certified public accountant has performed an independent audit of the company's records to ensure that the facts are accurately reported. An audited financial statement will be followed by a statement giving the opinion of the certified public accountant or accounting firm with regard to accuracy and fairness. In the absence of such a statement, the financial statements represent only the word of the company's management regarding its financial characteristics and profits.

Further study

The analysis in this chapter has focused on how to interpret the information in the financial statements. Further study would involve developing an understanding of how an accountant actually goes about recording transactions. Several good books for this purpose are:

Gibson, Charles, and Boyer, Patricia. *Financial Statement Analysis.* Boston: Addison-Wesley Publishing Co., 1979. 456 pages.

Each of the topics discussed briefly in the present chapter is discussed in detail by Gibson and Boyer. Their book focuses directly on the user of financial statements.

May, Robert; Mueller, Gerhard; and Williams, Thomas. *A New Introduction to Financial Accounting.* 2d. ed. Englewood Cliffs, N.J.: Prentice Hall, 1980. 797 pages.

This book would serve as an excellent handbook for someone who uses financial statements and needs a ready source dealing with the principles underlying any portion of the financial statements. This thorough treatment of the principles of accounting is written primarily for students of accounting.

Sweeny, Allen. *Accounting Fundamentals for Nonfinancial Executives.* New York: American Management Associations, 1972. 150 pages.

Sweeny provides a brief, nontechnical overview of the principles underlying financial statement preparation. The book provides a more thorough coverage than the present chapter without getting bogged down in detail.

3 Financial statement analysis

After learning how to read a financial statement, the next step is learning to analyze the information therein. Analysis of these statements can provide useful insights into what the company has done, both right and wrong, as well as yield predictions of company performance in coming years. Finally, through analysis of financial statements, managers can find ways to manage more effectively.

The purposes of financial statement analysis are many and varied. Financial statements are examined by potential trade creditors and bank officers considering short- and intermediate-term loans. They are also evaluated by long-term creditors, such as bondholders, as well as by the owners and managers of the company. Each user of financial statements will be interested in different types of information. Short-term creditors will be interested in the ability of the company to convert assets to cash in order to repay the debt within a short period of time. On the other hand, long-term creditors will be interested in the ability of the company to generate the necessary profits for repayment over a number of years. The creditors will also be interested in their own protection in the event a loan cannot be repaid. The owners are interested in both profitabiliy and safety of their investment. Finally, managers are interested in the profitability of the company, the efficiency with which assets are used, and the risk to which the company is exposed. Of course, managers must also be sensitive to how the financial statements will be viewed by the other interested parties.

As a first step in any analysis of financial statements, it is necessary to make the information comparable between two companies or between two years for the same company. As an example of the problem of comparability, suppose the profits for ABC company are 50 percent greater than those for XYZ company. Does this prove that the managers of ABC are more effective? To answer this question, other information is needed. If ABC had twice the assets and three times the owners' equity of XYZ, the shareholders would note that the profit-to-resources committed ratio was much lower for ABC, even though ABC's dollar profits were higher. The shareholders would not be interested in profit alone, but in the ratio of profit to something else, such as assets, sales, or owners' equity. The shareholders are not the only ones interested in relationships. The debt-to-total assets ratio frequently means more to a potential creditor than does the actual amount of debt. The focus in this chapter is on choosing helpful ratios and then using them to analyze the financial performance of the company.

Ratio analysis can be thought of as a diagnostic tool. Just as a doctor may take measurements of various characteristics of the blood, the person studying the company measures various relationships in the financial statements. A high or low value of some characteristics of the blood is seldom a disease in itself; it is more likely the symptom of a disease. Likewise, the study of financial statement ratios can yield symptoms of problems or of management errors, as well as pointing to possible solutions.

There are various categories of ratios. Liquidity ratios are used to measure the ability to meet cash obligations in the near future, and leverage ratios help in evaluating the use of debt. Activity ratios are used to evaluate the level of asset commitment and the efficiency of asset usage. Profitability ratios are used to evaluate the degree to which other activities result in profits. Market ratios measure the reactions of investors to the company's performance. By using ratios singly or in combination, it is possible to develop an understanding of the strengths and weaknesses of the company.

Liquidity ratios

Liquidity ratios are of particular interest to short-term creditors such as suppliers who have sold the company materials on credit and banks that have loaned the company money for short periods. Of course, the liquidity ratios are also of concern to financial managers who are responsible for ensuring that the company can meet its short-term obligations. The two primary liquidity ratios are the current ratio and the acid-test ratio.

Table 3–1 Office Supply Corporation

Income statements years ending December 31 (in millions)

	1980	*1981*	*1982*
Sales	$ 80	$100	$120
Cost of goods sold	40	50	60
Gross profit	40	50	60
Depreciation	5	6	8
Overhead expense	10	12	14
Sales expense	10	12	14
Net operating income	15	20	24
Interest	1	2	6
Earnings before taxes	14	18	18
Taxes	7	9	9
Net income	$ 7	$ 9	$ 9
Earnings per share	$0.70	$0.90	$0.90

Balance sheets December 31 (in millions)

Assets	*1980*	*1981*	*1982*
Cash	$ 8	$ 10	$ 10
Accounts receivable	16	20	58
Inventory	16	20	22
Total current assets	40	50	90
Fixed assets (net of depreciation)	40	50	60
Total assets	$ 80	$100	$150
Liabilities and net worth			
Accounts payable	$ 10	$ 15	$ 20
Miscellaneous accruals	10	15	20
Total current liabilities	20	30	40
Long-term debt	10	20	60
Common stock	10	10	10
Paid-in capital	10	10	10
Retained earnings	30	30	30
Total liabilities and net worth	$ 80	$100	$150

The current ratio is defined as current assets divided by current liabilities. Current assets consist primarily of cash, accounts receivable, and inventory, while current liabilities are those obligations that are due within one year. It is generally felt that those assets that the company expects to convert to cash within a short time should exceed the liabilities due in the near future by a comfortable margin. The current ratio is a measure of that margin. The financial statements of Office Supply Corporation appear in Table 3-1. For 1982, the current ratio was:

$$\text{current ratio} = \frac{\text{current assets}}{\text{current liabilities}} = \frac{90}{40} = 2.25$$

Table 3-2 shows Office Supply Corporation's current ratios for 1980 and 1981 as well as 1982. As a rule of thumb, it is frequently suggested that a company's current ratio should be at least 2.0. While one should not place too much weight on rules of thumb, the

Table 3-2 Financial ratios for Office Supply Corporation

	1980	*1981*	*1982*
Liquidity ratios			
Current ratio	2.00	1.67	2.25
Acid-test (quick) ratio	1.20	1.00	1.70
Leverage ratios			
Debt (debt-to-total assets) ratio	0.375	0.500	0.667
Debt-to-equity ratio	0.600	1.00	2.00
Times-interest-earned	15.0	10.0	4.0
Fixed charge coverage *	4.40	3.50	1.70
Activity ratios			
Inventory turnover ratio		2.78	2.86
Average collection period	73	73	176
Fixed asset turnover	2.00	2.00	2.00
Total asset turnover	1.00	1.00	0.80
Profitability ratios			
Net profit margin	0.088	0.090	0.075
Net return on assets	0.088	0.090	0.060
Operating profit margin	0.188	0.200	0.200
Operating return on assets	0.188	0.200	0.160
Return on equity	0.14	0.180	0.180
Market ratios			
Price-earnings ratio **	9.30	10.0	8.89
* Lease payment (in $ millions)	2.00	2.00	2.00
Debt repayment (in $ millions)	1.00	2.00	6.00
** Year-end stock price	$6.50	$9.00	$8.00

liquidity level of Office Supply meets the standard set by this rule as well as showing an increase from previous years.

The acid-test ratio (also called the quick ratio). Cash can be used to meet short-term obligations, and accounts receivable are normally converted to cash in a short time as customers pay their bills. However, it may be difficult to sell inventory quickly, particularly in periods of economic disturbance. Thus, the acid-test ratio is used to complement the current ratio by providing an additional look at liquidity. The formula and Office Supply's 1982 acid-test ratio are:

$$\text{acid-test ratio} = \frac{\text{current assets} - \text{inventory}}{\text{current liabilities}} = \frac{90 - 22}{40} = 1.70$$

An acid-test ratio of 1.0 is often considered a rule of thumb liquidity standard. By this standard, Office Supply is in a satisfactory liquidity position. In addition, Table 3–2 shows that Office Supply's acid-test ratio has increased over the past year and is above the level for either of the previous two years. Thus, the liquidity ratios do not point toward problems with regard to payment of short-term obligations.

Leverage ratios

The sources of money available to a company are divided between debt and equity. Debt, of course, is a fixed cost source of money. If the return on money employed in the business is greater than the interest rate on debt, the difference accrues to the equity holders. However, risk is increased by the use of debt financing because the company must meet debt obligations even if business conditions are bad. The leverage ratios (financial leverage ratios, to be more precise) give an indication of the extent of debt usage and the ability of the company to meet debt obligations. The leverage ratios used here are the debt ratio, times interest earned, and fixed charge coverage.

The debt ratio (also called the debt-to-total asset ratio) is defined as total debt divided by total assets. Total debt includes both the current liabilities and the long-term debt of the company. For 1982, Office Supply's debt ratio was:

$$\text{debt ratio} = \frac{\text{total debt}}{\text{total assets}} = \frac{100}{150} = 0.667$$

Table 3–2 shows that the debt ratio has increased substantially over the three-year period. In 1980, only 37.5 percent of the assets were financed by debt, but by 1982, two-thirds of the assets were financed by debt. Looked at another way, the creditors would have recovered all of their funds in a 1980 bankruptcy if the assets could have been sold for at least 37.5 percent of their book value. By 1982, the assets would need to be sold at two-thirds of their book value for the creditors to recover their funds. The creditors would want to look at some other factors as well, but the rapid increase in the percentage of assets financed by debt would be cause for concern and further questions.

The debt-to-equity ratio is another frequently used leverage measure. As its name implies, it is the ratio of total debt to stockholders' equity. For Office Supply Corporation, the owners' equity consists of common stock, paid-in capital, and retained earnings. The 1982 debt-to-equity ratio was:

$$\text{debt-to-equity ratio} = \frac{\text{total debt}}{\text{owners' equity}} = \frac{100}{50} = 2.0$$

The debt-to-equity ratio is actually redundant if the debt-to-total asset ratio has been computed since the two ratios convey the same information. The debt-to-equity ratio is mentioned here because publications providing industry average ratios for comparison frequently cite the debt-to-equity ratio instead of the debt-to-total assets ratio. Thus, it is necessary to be familiar with other measures.

The debt-to-total asset and debt-to-equity ratios are comparisons of two stocks: the stock of assets and the stock of debt. They provide measures of the creditors' protection in the event of bankruptcy. However, few loans are granted on the basis of the protection the creditor will have if the borrower defaults; loans are made only if the lender feels the borrower has an adequate flow of funds to meet loan commitments. Likewise, a company normally would not want to borrow money if it did not have the means of repayment available. The times-interest-earned and fixed charge coverage ratios are measures of ability to repay.

The-times-interest-earned ratio compares interest expense to income available to meet that expense. It is the ratio of earnings before interest and taxes (EBIT) to interest expense. EBIT is found by adding interest expense back to the company's earnings before tax. Office Supply's 1982 times-interest-earned was:

$$\text{times-interest-earned} = \frac{\text{EBIT}}{\text{interest}} = \frac{18 + 6}{6} = 4.0$$

In other words, income before deduction of interest expense could fall to one-fourth of its present level and Office Supply Corporation would still have income equal to its interest expenses. Although this ratio has declined from previous years, it is still not terribly low. The trend in this ratio would be of greater concern than its absolute level at the moment.

The times-interest-earned ratio complements the debt-to-total assets ratio in providing additional information about the company's ability to meet debt obligations. However, it still does not present a complete picture. The ultimate question is one of whether or not the company can meet cash commitments to creditors. Thus, a ratio based on cash flows is helpful.

The fixed charge coverage ratio is a measure of the ratio of cash flow available for meeting financing charges to total flows required to meet those obligations. The formula for the fixed charge coverage ratio is:

$$\text{fixed charge coverage} = \frac{\text{earnings before tax} + \text{depreciation} + \text{interest} + \text{lease payment}}{\text{interest} + \text{lease payment} + \text{debt repayment}/(1 - \text{tax rate})}$$

In this formula, interest expense and lease payments are added to earnings before tax to yield earnings before financing charges. Because depreciation was deducted from sales revenue to compute net income even though it is not a cash expense, adding it back gives a rough estimate of *cash flow* available to service debt. Debt repayment is adjusted for taxes in the formula because it is not an expense for tax purposes and must therefore be paid from after-tax cash flows.

As pointed out in Table 3–2, 1982 lease payments for Office Supply were \$2 million and scheduled debt repayment was \$6 million. Thus, the 1982 fixed charge coverage ratio was:

$$\text{fixed charge coverage} = \frac{18 + 8 + 6 + 2}{6 + 2 + 6/(1 - 0.5)} = \frac{34}{20} = 1.7$$

Debt has been increased to the point where cash flows available to meet fixed financing charges are only 1.7 times those charges. Table 3–2 shows that this is a significant decline from the levels of previous years. In fact, the fixed charge coverage was cut in half in a one-year period.

The leverage ratios illustrate the effect debt financing has on the risk faced by Office Supply Corporation and its creditors. The income and cash flows available to meet financing charges have not kept pace with the rapid increase in financing charges. If this trend continues, the company will not be able to meet its obligations to creditors. The debt ratio also shows that the creditors' margin of protection in the event of a default has declined; assets would have to be sold for at least two-thirds of their book value if the creditors were to recover their money. This situation would cause concern for both the creditors and the company's managers.

Activity ratios

Activity ratios are used to measure the efficiency of asset use. The activity ratios discussed here are inventory turnover, average collection period, fixed asset turnover, and total asset turnover.

Inventory turnover is the ratio of the cost of goods sold to average inventory. The average inventory for a year is normally computed as the average of the ending inventory and beginning inventory (ending inventory for the previous year). For 1982, Office Supply's average inventory was (20 + 22)/2 = 21. The inventory turnover for 1982 was:

$$\text{inventory turnover} = \frac{\text{cost of goods sold}}{\text{average inventory}} = \frac{60}{21} = 2.86$$

In other words, the average piece of inventory was held 128 days (365/2.86) before it was sold. Table 3–2 shows that inventory turnover has increased somewhat from 1981, indicating that less inventory was needed for each dollar of sales. The primary thing this tells us is that relatively less funds are tied up in inventory. If a pattern of decreasing inventory turnover had been observed, there would be questions about excessive funds tied up in inventory as well as the possibility of obsolete inventory that must eventually be sold at a loss.

When comparing inventory turnover ratios from one company to another company or to industry averages, the accounting methods used to value inventory should be taken into account. As was discussed in Chapter 2, the value of inventory can be significantly affected by the choice between LIFO (last-in, first-out) and FIFO (first-in, first-out) accounting methods. When comparing inventory turnover for two companies, it is necessary to determine if they are using the same accounting methods.

Other problems involve the exact method used to compute inventory turnover. Ending inventory is sometimes used instead of average inventory and the ratio of sales to inventory is sometimes used instead of the ratio of cost of goods sold to inventory. When comparing a company to the industry averages, it is important to use the same formula used to compute the industry average ratios.

The average collection period indicates the average number of days between the sale of a product and the receipt of payment. The formula for computation and Office Supply's 1982 average collection period is:

$$\text{average collection period} = 365 \times \frac{\text{accounts receivable}}{\text{sales}}$$

$$= 365 \times \frac{58}{120} = 176 \text{ days}$$

Table 3–2 shows that the average collection period was 73 days in each of the previous two years. If Office Supply Corporation was selling its products on 60-day credit terms, this would indicate that the average bill was paid 13 days after it was due in the two previous years. That is not an unusually long delay and would not have caused concern. However, an increase to 176 days in 1982 would indicate that unless credit terms have changed, the average customer is now more than 100 days late in paying. Since the company must pay interest for the use of money, these uncollected receivables reduce its profits. Furthermore, the fact that these receivables are several months past due raises questions as to whether they will ever be collected.

The average collection period also provides an illustration of how ratios can be used in combination to develop a better understanding of the company's financial strength. The current ratio and acid-test ratio looked satisfactory, indicating that the company probably would be able to meet its current obligations. However, the long average collection period raises serious questions about the quality of the current assets. A high current ratio is of little comfort if the current assets are of such poor quality that a large proportion of them may never be converted to cash. Questions about reported profits are also being raised since sales may never be converted to cash.

The fixed asset turnover ratio is a measure of the sales generated per dollar of fixed assets. The formula and the 1982 fixed asset turnover ratio for Office Supply Corporation are:

$$\text{fixed asset turnover} = \frac{\text{sales}}{\text{fixed assets}} = \frac{120}{60} = 2.0$$

Office Supply's fixed asset turnover has remained constant, indicating that efficiency of fixed asset usage has neither increased nor decreased.

One point of caution is necessary with regard to the interpretation of this ratio. When comparing the performance of companies, it is necessary to consider the age of the fixed assets. If a company has new factories, its fixed asset turnover would be expected to be much lower than that of a company with old, fully depreciated factories. This would not necessarily mean that the company with old factories was doing a better job as it might be giving up efficiency by using older equipment.

The total asset turnover ratio is a summary measure of the efficiency of asset usage. It is a measure of sales generated per dollar of assets committed. The formula and the 1982 total asset turnover for Office Supply are:

$$\text{total asset turnover} = \frac{\text{sales}}{\text{total assets}} = \frac{120}{150} = 0.80$$

As shown in Table 3–2, the total asset turnover has declined from 1981 to 1982. This comes as no surprise since the day's receivables outstanding increased so dramatically and there were no offsetting decreases in other assets. Taken together, the activity ratios show us that Office Supply Corporation is not using its assets as efficiently as in years past.

Profitability ratios

Profitability ratios are used to measure the ability of the company to turn sales into profits and to earn profits on funds committed. The first set of profitability ratios examined here compares profit to sales; the second set compares profit to assets committed; and the final profitability ratio compares profit to the owners' investment.

The net profit margin is an indicator of the company's ability to convert sales to profit after taxes. The formula and Office Supply's 1982 net profit margin are:

$$\text{net profit margin} = \frac{\text{profit after tax}}{\text{sales}} = \frac{9}{120} = 0.075$$

The net profit margin increased from 1980 to 1981, but decreased from 1981 to 1982. Overall, the company was not able to earn as much profit per dollar of sales in 1982 as in the previous two years. From the perspective of the owners and managers, this is a matter of concern.

The net profit margin has a limitation in that it is based on income after deduction of interest expense. If the company has increased its debt-to-equity ratio substantially, this may result in a decrease in the net profit margin because of the interest expense deduction, even if the return on the owners' equity investment has actually increased. The operating profit margin overcomes this problem and provides another view of profitability.

The operating profit margin is based on earnings generated before allowance for financing expense. Thus, it reflects only results from operations and is not affected by financing costs or changes in financial structure. The formula and the 1982 operating profit margin for Office Supply are:

$$\text{operating profit margin} = \frac{\text{net operating income}}{\text{sales}} = \frac{24}{120} = 0.20$$

As Table 3–2 shows, the operating profit margin remained steady from 1981 to 1982 while the net profit margin decreased. In other words, the operating income per dollar of sales remained constant while increased financing costs caused the net profit margin to decline.

The net return on assets measures profit in relation to assets committed rather than in relation to sales. Thus, it might be viewed as a measure of the efficiency of asset usage. The net return on assets is simply the profit after tax divided by total assets. The formula and Office Supply's 1982 net return on assets are:

$$\text{net return on assets} = \frac{\text{profit after tax}}{\text{total assets}} = \frac{9}{150} = 0.06$$

Like the net profit margin, the net return on assets increased slightly from 1980 to 1981, and then declined sharply. However, this ratio alone does not tell us if the decline resulted from an inability to generate operating returns or from increased financing costs resulting from an increase in the proportion of assets financed by debt. The next ratio aids in pinpointing the cause of the decline.

The operating return on assets (also known as earning power) is the ratio of net operating income to total assets.[1] The formula and Office Supply's 1982 ratio are:

$$\text{operating return on assets} = \frac{\text{net operating income}}{\text{total assets}} = \frac{24}{150} = 0.16$$

The operating return on assets increased from 1980 to 1981, indicating an increased ability to earn returns from assets. However,

---

[1] Operating assets are used instead of total assets if the firm has a large volume of nonoperating assets such as securities.

this ability was not maintained in 1982. The decline in profit per dollar of assets *before* considering the cost of financing indicates that the problem is one of inefficient asset usage and not simply the result of a change in the debt-to-equity ratio.

The return on equity (also known as return on net worth) shows the cumulative effect of all other factors affecting profitability. This is the return on the investment of the common shareholders. It is the ratio of profit after tax (less preferred dividends if there is preferred stock outstanding) to owners' equity. As is typical of most companies, Office Supply's equity accounts consist of common stock plus paid-in capital plus retained earnings. Office Supply's return on equity for 1982 was:

$$\text{return on equity} = \frac{\text{profit after tax}}{\text{equity}} = \frac{9}{10 + 10 + 30} = 0.18$$

Note that although the operating return on assets and net return on assets declined, the return on equity remained constant. This occurred because the decrease in return on assets was offset by the financing of a greater proportion of total assets with debt. Because the debt has a fixed cost which is lower than the operating return on assets in this case, the difference in earnings accrued to the equity, leaving the return on the owners' investment constant. Consequently, profitability was maintained at the expense of increased risk as the company experienced a deterioration in all of its leverage ratios.

Market ratios

Market ratios are used to study the way investors and stock markets have reacted to the company's performance. The most widely used market ratio is the *price-earnings ratio*. It is simply the ratio of the market price of the stock to the earnings per share (net income divided by number of shares). The price of Office Supply's stock was \$8.00 per share at the end of 1982. This gives a price-earnings ratio of:

$$\text{price-earnings ratio} = \frac{\text{market price}}{\text{earnings per share}} = \frac{8.00}{0.90} = 8.89$$

Table 3–2 shows that the price-earnings ratio increased from 1980 to 1981 and then declined from 1981 to 1982. The increase in 1981 probably resulted from optimism caused by an increase in sales, earnings per share, return on equity, etc. However, the 1982 figures were most likely disappointing to investors. Although sales increased and the operating profit margin on these sales remained constant, assets were used inefficiently. This resulted in no increase in earnings per share or return on equity and in a decline in the leverage ratios. Investors saw risk increase while return remained constant.

Sources of comparative ratios

In the example followed in this chapter, the company's ratios for 1982 were mostly compared to its ratios for previous years. This is a particularly useful approach because the company's historical data may be more comparable than data for other firms with different characteristics and different accounting methods. However, it is frequently desirable to supplement an analysis of ratio trends with a comparison to other companies.

The most common approach to comparison with other companies is to use industry average ratios. Dunn and Bradstreet, the commercial credit reporting company, publishes an annual pamphlet entitled *Key Business Ratios.* This pamphlet contains representative industry average ratios for over one hundred lines of business. It is normally furnished free on request at local offices of Dunn and Bradstreet.

Robert Morris Associates, the association of bank lending officers, publishes a book entitled *Statement Studies,* which includes industry average ratios for over 150 lines of business. The Federal Trade Commission publishes *Quarterly Financial Report for Manufacturing Corporations,* which is another useful source.

In addition to these sources of published industry ratios, many industry associations provide industry average ratios and other statistics for their particular industry. These are made available to association members, frequently for a fee.

A final source of comparative statistics is the study of financial statements of other companies. Many managers compare the financial performance of their companies to that of the industry leader or to that of several of their leading competitors. The advantage of selecting several individual companies for comparison is that one can choose the companies that are similar to his own firm in characteristics such as size, and also allows one to check their reports for differences in accounting practices which might render such comparisons meaningless.

Summary

The use of ratios to determine the financial strengths and weaknesses of a company has been illustrated in this chapter. The most widely used ratios are summarized in Table 3–3. Used individually, the ratios allow one to look in detail at specific aspects of a company's financial performance. Used in combination, the ratios serve as powerful diagnostic tools. The discussions in the remainder of this book will illustrate the importance of financial statement analysis for all phases of financial decision making.

Solved problems

Problem 1 Johnson Fabricating presently has no long-term debt and no lease commitments. However, the company does have $40,000 of short-term bank debt outstanding in addition to $16,000 of accounts payable. The bank has encouraged the company to replace the short-term loan with the long-term debt, and your firm has been approached as a possible long-term lender. Johnson proposes paying off the loan in ten annual installments of $4,000 each. The loan would carry an 8 percent annual interest rate which is the same rate charged by the bank. The company faces a 20 percent tax rate. Following are certain historical data and industry average ratios for 1978.

Year	*1975*	*1976*	*1977*	*1978*	*1979*
Sales	$100,000	$110,000	$125,000	$140,000	$160,000
Depreciation	10,000	11,000	12,000	14,000	16,000
Net operating income	15,000	18,000	21,000	25,000	30,000
Interest expense	2,000	2,200	2,500	2,800	3,200
Total assets	80,000	88,000	100,000	112,000	128,000
Accounts payable	10,000	11,000	12,500	14,000	16,000
Bank notes	25,000	27,500	31,250	35,000	40,000
Net worth	45,000	49,500	56,250	63,000	72,000

Table 3–3 Key financial ratios

Ratio	Formula
Liquidity ratios	
current ratio	$\dfrac{\text{current assets}}{\text{current liabilities}}$
acid-test ratio (quick ratio)	$\dfrac{\text{current assets} - \text{inventory}}{\text{current liabilities}}$
Leverage ratios	
debt ratio (debt-to-total assets)	$\dfrac{\text{total debt}}{\text{total assets}}$
times-interest-earned	$\dfrac{\text{earnings before taxes} + \text{interest}}{\text{interest}}$
fixed charge coverage	$\dfrac{\text{earnings before taxes} + \text{depreciation} + \text{interest} + \text{lease payment}}{\text{interest} + \text{lease payment} + \text{debt repayment}/(1 - \text{tax rate})}$
Activity ratios	
inventory turnover	$\dfrac{\text{cost of goods sold}}{\text{average inventory}}$
average collection period	$365 \times \dfrac{\text{accounts receivable}}{\text{sales}}$
fixed asset turnover	$\dfrac{\text{sales}}{\text{fixed assets}}$
total asset turnover	$\dfrac{\text{sales}}{\text{total assets}}$
Profitability ratios	
net profit margin	$\dfrac{\text{profit after taxes}}{\text{sales}}$
operating profit margin	$\dfrac{\text{net operating income}}{\text{sales}}$
net return on assets	$\dfrac{\text{profit after taxes}}{\text{total assets}}$
operating return on assets	$\dfrac{\text{net operating income}}{\text{total assets}}$
return on equity	$\dfrac{\text{profit after taxes}}{\text{equity}}$
Market ratios	
price-earnings ratio	$\dfrac{\text{market price of stock}}{\text{earnings per share}}$

Industry average ratios for 1978

Operating profit margin	*Total asset turnover*	*Times interest earned*	*Debt ratio*	*Net profit margin*	*Fixed charge coverage*	*Operating return on assets*
20.0%	1.25	10.6	0.42	9.4%	4.5	25.0%

a. Compute the appropriate ratios for analysis from the position of a long-term creditor.

b. Would you recommend that the loan be approved?

Solution

a. *Year*	*1975*	*1976*	*1977*	*1978*	*1979*	*Industry*
Leverage						
Times-interest-earned	7.5	8.2	8.4	8.9	9.4	10.6
Fixed charge coverage					5.6*	4.5
Debt ratio	0.44	0.44	0.44	0.44	0.44	0.42
Activity						
Total asset turnover	1.25	1.25	1.25	1.25	1.25	1.25
Profitability						
Operating profit margin	0.15	0.16	0.17	0.18	0.19	0.20
Operating return on assets	0.19	0.20	0.21	0.22	0.23	0.25
Net profit margin	0.10	0.11	0.12	0.13	0.13	0.094

* Assuming the loan repayment schedule had been in effect in 1979.

b. While information about the liquidity position is not given, we can assume a low current ratio in light of the fact that all debt is short-term. Total asset turnover has remained at the same level as the industry average while leverage and profitability ratios present a mixed picture. Operating profitability ratios are below the industry average and net profit margin is above it. Likewise, the times-interest-earned ratio is below the industry average while the fixed charge coverage ratio is above it. In light of a debt ratio equal to the industry average, these apparent anomalies may arise from the relatively small size and resulting low tax rate of the company. An important consideration here is the steady improvement in profitability and leverage ratios and the relatively small deviations from the industry averages. Based on the information given, the company looks like a good loan candidate. It should be noted, however, that continued growth will result in a need for increased debt.

Problem 2 Gillespie Cotton Fabrics, Inc. has suffered a decline in liquidity. Compute the appropriate ratios from the information shown below, identify the problem, and suggest corrective action.

Year	*1975*	*1976*	*1977*	*1978*	*1979*
Sales	$100	$110	$120	$130	$140
Accounts receivable	30	33	38	44	50
Inventory	50	55	60	65	70
Total current assets	90	99	110	122	134
Current liabilities	40	49	60	72	84

Solution

Year	*1975*	*1976*	*1977*	*1978*	*1979*
Current ratio	2.25	2.02	1.83	1.69	1.60
Acid-test ratio	1.00	0.90	0.83	0.79	0.76
Days' receivables outstanding	109	109	116	124	130
Sales to ending inventory *	2.0	2.0	2.0	2.0	2.0

Inventory has grown only at the same rate as sales and current assets, other than accounts receivable and inventory, have grown at the same rate as sales. Only accounts receivable have grown faster. The accounts receivable level is obviously one problem.

Reworking the statements to see what would have happened if current asset turnover had remained at the 1975 level reveals another problem. If current asset turnover were raised to the 1975 level, current assets would be reduced by $8. If the $8 were used to reduce current liabilities, the current ratio would only increase to 126 ÷ 76 = 1.66, and the acid-test ratio would only increase to 56 ÷ 76 = 0.74. Another important problem, then, is the growing level of current liabilities. All the growth in current assets has been financed through current liabilities. To improve the liquidity position, it appears that a shift to more long-term financing is required.

4
Profitability analysis

Profitability is the unifying theme of finance. Investors seek opportunities that provide the most profitable use of their funds. In order to compete for investors' funds, corporations must find the most profitable opportunities available. This continual drive for profitability serves to allocate society's resources and provides constant motivation to both profit and nonprofit organizations. This chapter covers ways to measure and improve profitability.

Profit vs. profitability

If you invested $1 million and earned a profit of $1,000, you would certainly be unhappy with your return. On the other hand, someone who earned $1,000 on an investment of $2,000 would probably be quite pleased. Obviously, the amount of profit itself is not a very meaningful number; it must be measured in relation to the level of activity or the amount of money committed.

Since profit is ultimately viewed from the owners' standpoint, the most direct measure of profitability is the ratio of profit to the owners' investment that is necessary to generate that profit. This is the *return on equity* ratio first introduced in Chapter 3. The financial statements for Midstate Box Company appear in Table 4–1. Midstate's return on equity for 1981 was:

$$\text{return on equity} = \frac{\text{profit after taxes}}{\text{owners' equity}} = \frac{24}{100 + 200} = 8.00\%$$

Table 4–1 Midstate Box Company

Income statement
year ending December 31
(000,000 omitted)

	1981	*1982*
Sales	$1,000	$1,100
Cost of goods sold	700	785
Gross profit	300	315
Administration and overhead	230	240
Net operating income	70	75
Interest expense	30	30
Earnings before taxes	40	45
Income taxes	16	18
Net income	24	27
Earnings per share	0.24	0.27

Balance sheet
December 31
(000,000 omitted)

	1981	*1982*
Cash	$ 25	$ 25
Accounts receivable	110	110
Inventory	165	185
Total current assets	300	320
Fixed assets	300	300
Total assets	600	620
Accounts payable	$ 25	$ 32
Miscellaneous accruals	10	13
Short-term bank debt	15	15
Total current liabilities	50	60
Long-term debt	250	250
Common stock ($1 par)	100	100
Retained earnings	200	210
Total liabilities and net worth	$600	$620

By way of comparison, the return on equity was 8.71 percent (27/310) in 1982. Thus, profitability increased from 1981 to 1982.

Return on equity is occasionally criticized on the grounds that the book or accounting value of owners' equity may not represent the true value of their investment. A company might own land that was purchased years ago and is still carried at original cost rather than current value. To make meaningful comparisons between companies, it is sometimes necessary to recompute owners' equity to equal the current value of the firm's assets minus its liabilities.

The profit margin on sales is sometimes suggested as a general profitability measure; however, it does not compare profit to resources committed. Some companies have high profit margins *and* low profitability because they use high investment in assets, and require high investment by owners for each dollar of sales.

The earnings yield—the ratio of earnings per share of common stock to market price per share—is also occasionally suggested as a general profitability measure. Because it is a measure of the return available to the shareholder, the earnings yield is of interest to investors. However, it is not a good measure of company performance. The earnings yield of a company that is very profitable may be even lower than that of an unprofitable competitor because the price of the profitable company's stock has been bid up in the marketplace while the price of the competitor's stock has fallen.

While these other profitability measures have their uses, they do not serve as overall measures of profitability. Only return on equity can serve as a unifying measure of profitability.

Earning power system

For profitability analysis to be most useful, it must provide insights into how profitability can be improved; furthermore, it must aid in identifying the various factors affecting profitability. The system for doing this is explained in the following paragraphs.

Profitability can be affected by both the financing decisions—the methods used to raise funds to acquire assets—and the operating decisions of nonfinancial managers. As a beginning step in profitability analysis, it is helpful to separate the effects of operating decisions from the effects of financing decisions. The earning power system focuses entirely on the operating performance of the firm, i.e., the efficiency with which resources are used without reference to how those resources were acquired. Later in this chapter, the interaction of financing and operating decisions is examined.

Earning power analysis begins with the operating return on assets (net operating income/total assets), which is frequently referred to as the *earning power* ratio. This ratio, which measures the ability to generate profits from assets, is affected by two other relationships: the operating profit per dollar of sales (operating profit margin) and the sales per dollar of assets (turnover). Specifically, the relationship is:[1]

$$\text{earning power} = \frac{\text{net operating income}}{\text{sales}} \times \frac{\text{sales}}{\text{total assets}}$$

or

$$\text{earning power} = \text{operating profit margin} \times \text{total asset turnover}$$

As this analysis shows, margin and turnover act together to generate a return on assets. The earning power relationship makes possible a focus on two factors affecting profitability: the ability to use assets to generate sales and the ability to convert sales to profits. The usefulness of the earning power relationship can be illustrated by comparing 1981 and 1982 earning power:

	earning power	=	margin	×	turnover
1981	11.67%	=	7.00%	×	1.667
1982	12.10%	=	6.82%	×	1.774

In 1982, the company generated less profit per dollar of sales, as illustrated by the decrease in operating profit margin from 7.00 percent to 6.82 percent; however, the company generated more sales per dollar of assets. This increase in sales per dollar of assets more than offset the decrease in profit per dollar of sales, resulting in an increase in profitability. Hence, the earning power system is particularly helpful as a diagnostic tool. For example, the management of Midstate Box could look at this relationship and decide that while they were happy with the turnover situation, they would like to improve the margins to increase profitability further.

An advantage of the basic earning power approach is that it can be easily extended for an examination not only of these components of profitability, but also of the factors that affect them. Figure 4-1

[1] Occasionally a company will have a substantial volume of assets such as bonds or stock in other companies that are not used in the running of the business. In these cases, operating assets—defined as assets actually used to carry out the company's business—are sometimes used instead of total assets.

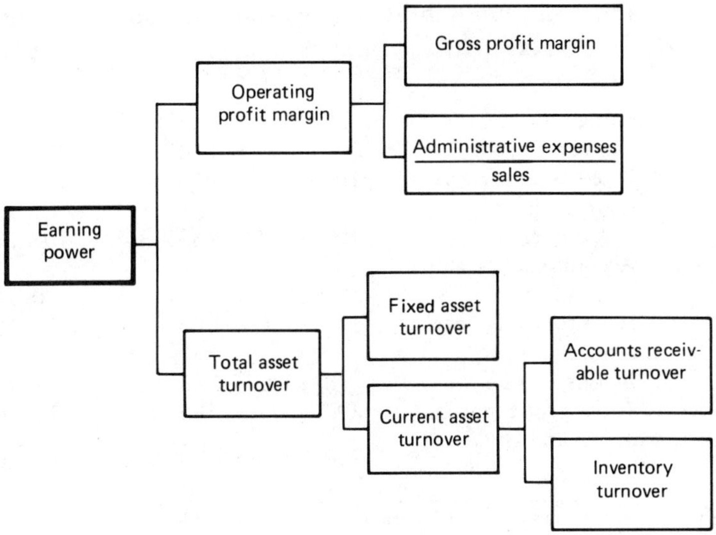

Figure 4–1 Earning power system

shows how the earning power system can be expanded to provide a full profitability analysis system. It also highlights the factors affecting margin and turnover as well as the interaction between these two factors.

Table 4–2 illustrates the profitability analysis computations used in connection with Figure 4–1. Again indicated is the fact that earning power has increased because the increase in turnover more than offset the decrease in margin. The analysis also highlights the factors leading to the increase in turnover: both the fixed asset turnover and the current asset turnover increased. The increase in accounts receivable turnover lead to the improvement in current asset turnover, which more than offset a small decrease in inventory turnover. Thus, a manager seeking even more efficient use of assets would probably focus on inventory turnover first, to see what caused the decline in turnover and to determine what could be done to improve it.

For Midstate Box Company, only two accounts that affect margin are shown. These are the cost of goods sold (or the related gross profit) and the administrative and overhead expense category. The gross profit margin declined, indicating that the cost of goods sold increased at a faster rate than did sales. Although administrative and overhead expenses decreased in relations to sales, the decrease was not enough to offset the decline in the gross profit margin. The result was an overall decrease in the operating profit margin. Under such a

Table 4-2 Profitability analysis of Midstate Box Company

Year	*1981*	*1982*
Earning power	70/600 = 11.67%	75/620 = 12.10%
Turnover	1000/600 = 1.667	1100/620 = 1.774
Fixed asset turnover	1000/300 = 3.333	1100/300 = 3.667
Current asset turnover	1000/300 = 3.333	1100/320 = 3.438
Accounts receivable turnover	1000/110 = 9.091	1100/110 = 10.000
Inventory turnover*	1000/165 = 6.06	1100/185 = 5.95
Operating profit margin	70/1000 = 7.00%	75/1100 = 6.82%
Gross profit margin	300/1000 = 30.00%	315/1100 = 28.64%
Admin. and Overhead / Sales	230/1000 = 23.00%	240/1100 = 21.82%

*Based on sales ÷ year-end inventory

circumstance, a manager would be expected to examine the factors that led to the decline in the gross profit margin as well as possible remedies for the decline.

The earning power system serves two purposes with regard to operating decisions. First, it allows us to measure the past profitability of the company along with the profitability of several different areas of responsibility. Second, and probably more important, it serves as a powerful diagnostic tool: it does not necessarily explain why profitability has increased or decreased, but it allows us to quickly locate the areas of operations that have led to an increase or decrease. The manager can then focus on these particular areas to determine what has happened and what can be done to improve profitability.

Financial leverage and profitability

Financial leverage analysis is the part of the profitability analysis that focuses directly on the contribution of the financial manager through efficient financing of resources. Financial leverage refers to the use of fixed cost sources of financing such as debt, preferred stock, and leases, and the use of spontaneous sources of funds such as accounts payable and accrued expenses. If the return on owners' equity is higher than it would have been if all assets were financed by owners' equity, the company is using *favorable* financial leverage.

The impact of financial leverage can be measured through the *total financial leverage* (TFL). The TFL is the ratio of before-tax return on equity to earning power. A TFL greater than 1.0 indicates favorable financial leverage. The TFL formula and Midstate's total financial leverage for 1981 and 1982 are:[2]

$$\text{total financial leverage} = \frac{\text{before tax return on equity}}{\text{earning power}}$$

$$1981\ \text{TFL} = \frac{40/300}{70/600} = \frac{0.1333}{0.1167} = 1.142$$

$$1982\ \text{TFL} = \frac{45/310}{75/620} = \frac{0.1452}{0.1210} = 1.200$$

Regarding Midstate Box in particular, we see that the TFL was higher in 1982 than in 1981, indicating that financial leverage made a greater contribution to profitability in 1982 than in 1981.

The total financial leverage equation can be rewritten as:

$$\text{before-tax return on equity} = \text{earning power} \times \text{TFL}$$

This formulation emphasizes both the potential benefits and the limitations of proper financing decisions. Since TFL is simply a multiplier applied to earning power, it can amplify profitability; however, it cannot create profitability where none existed.

Break-even analysis

Break-even analysis examines the relationship between profit and sales levels, and because it is an analysis of the potential effects on profit by changes in the sales level, it is a useful supplement to profit-

[2]If a company has preferred stock outstanding, the formula becomes a bit more complicated because preferred stock is really a fixed cost method of financing and should not be included as part of owners' equity. The correct formula becomes:

$$\text{TFL} = \frac{\dfrac{\text{earnings before tax} - \dfrac{\text{preferred dividends}}{1 - \text{marginal tax rate}}}{\text{stockholders' investment} - \text{preferred stock}}}{\text{earning power}}$$

ability analysis. In addition, break-even analysis yields useful information for estimating the company's degree of risk exposure.

Costs can be divided into two primary types: variable and fixed. *Variable costs*, such as raw materials, shipping expenses, and production labor, change as the level of output changes. A *fixed cost*, on the other hand, remains the same regardless of the level of output. Examples of fixed costs are depreciation, administrative salaries, and interest expense. The impacts of fixed costs are frequently referred to as leverage. Operating leverage refers to the impact of fixed operating expenses such as depreciation; financial leverage refers to the impact of fixed financing costs such as interest.

Break-even analysis is useful for deciding the likelihood of success for a new business. Consider, for example, a proposed retail store. Fixed costs for the store will be \$5,000 per month. Merchandise is expected to cost an average of 75 percent of its selling price. From this, the sales needed each month to break even can be quickly determined. The break-even point formula[3] and the store's break-even point are:

$$\text{break-even point} = \frac{\text{fixed costs}}{1 - \text{variable costs as a \% of sales}}$$

$$\text{break-even point} = \frac{\$5{,}000}{1 - 0.75} = \$20{,}000$$

If the new business is to break even, it must generate sales of \$20,000 per month. The person considering opening this business can compare the sales potential to this break-even point.

A break-even chart is an excellent method for graphic analysis of profit potential. The break-even chart in Figure 4–2 shows the total cost and the total revenue at each possible level of sales for the store.

In preparing the break-even chart, the first step is to draw a 45° line representing total revenue. Next, the total cost line is found by determining the fixed costs that occur even if there are no sales (\$5,000 in this case) and the total cost at any one level of sales. For example, total costs at \$30,000 of sales would be \$5,000 + 0.75 × \$30,000 = \$27,500. When these two points have been identified on the chart, a line passing through both of them represents the total cost at each level of sales. The difference between the total cost and

---

[3] Sometimes it is preferable to state the break-even point in units sold rather than dollars. The unit formula is:

$$\text{unit break-even point} = \frac{\text{fixed costs}}{\text{price per unit} - \text{variable cost per unit}}$$

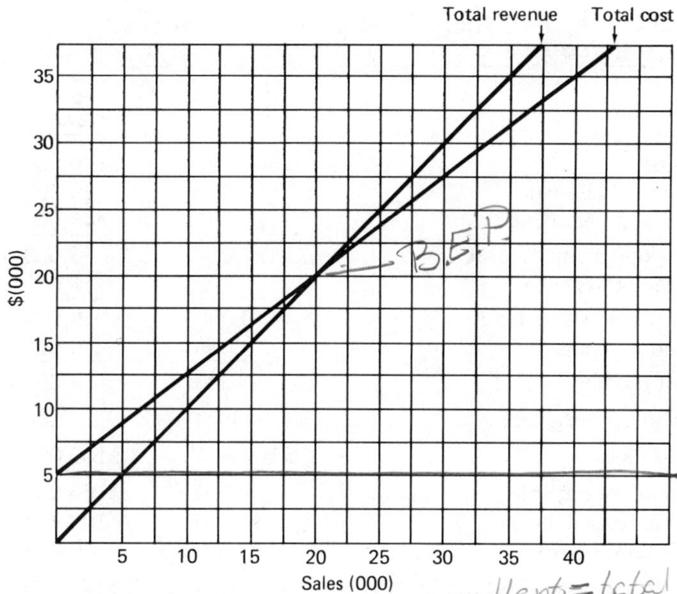

Figure 4–2 Break-even chart

total revenue lines represents profit. Below sales of $20,000, total cost exceeds total revenue and the company experiences a loss. Above sales of $20,000, total revenue exceeds total cost, with the difference between the two lines representing a profit. One can simply look at this chart to predict the profit at any level of sales.

Break-even analysis is also useful for problems such as choosing among alternate production and promotion strategies. For example, another company, FAU Inc., has available two methods of production: one labor intensive and the other capital intensive. The labor intensive approach involves high variable costs as a percentage of sales and low fixed costs; whereas, the capital intensive approach has high fixed costs in the form of depreciation and interest expense, but has low variable costs. The financial statements in Table 4–3 show an abbreviated company financial statement as it would appear with each production method. While both production methods provide the same profit and earnings per share at sales of $100,000, the high-leverage option has lower variable costs as a percent of sales (30 percent versus 60 percent) and higher fixed costs. If sales increase, profit will increase more rapidly with the high-leverage option. However, profit will also decline more rapidly with the high-leverage option if sales decline.

Table 4–3 FAU Inc. cost structure alternatives

	Low leverage	*High leverage*
Sales	$100,000	$100,000
Variable costs	60,000	20,000
Fixed operating costs	20,000	45,000
Net operating income	20,000	35,000
Interest expense	0	15,000
Earnings before taxes	20,000	20,000
Income taxes	10,000	10,000
Net income	10,000	10,000
Earnings per share	1.00	1.00
Total assets	$100,000	$100,000
Accounts payable	$ 50,000	$ 50,000
Long-term debt	0	100,000
Owners' equity	50,000	50,000
Total liabilities and net worth	$100,000	$200,000

The break-even point is one measure of the risk-return characteristics of the two options. The break-even points under the two options are:

$$\text{low-leverage BEP} = \frac{20{,}000}{1 - 0.6} = \$50{,}000$$

$$\text{high-leverage BEP} = \frac{45{,}000 + 15{,}000}{1 - 0.2} = \$75{,}000$$

At a sales level above $75,000, the company will earn a profit with either production method. Between $50,000 and $75,000 of sales, the company will earn a profit with the low-leverage production method, but not with the high-leverage option. Thus, the high-leverage option is more risky. However, as sales rise higher and higher, the extra risk of accepting a higher break-even point is rewarded with higher profitability.

An indifference chart is also helpful in evaluating alternatives of this type. An indifference chart for the two alternate production methods appears in Figure 4–3. The indifference chart shows the profit before tax at each level of sales for each production method. It can be used to quickly determine the profitability of each production method at each sales level and to determine the sales level above which the high-leverage option would be preferred.

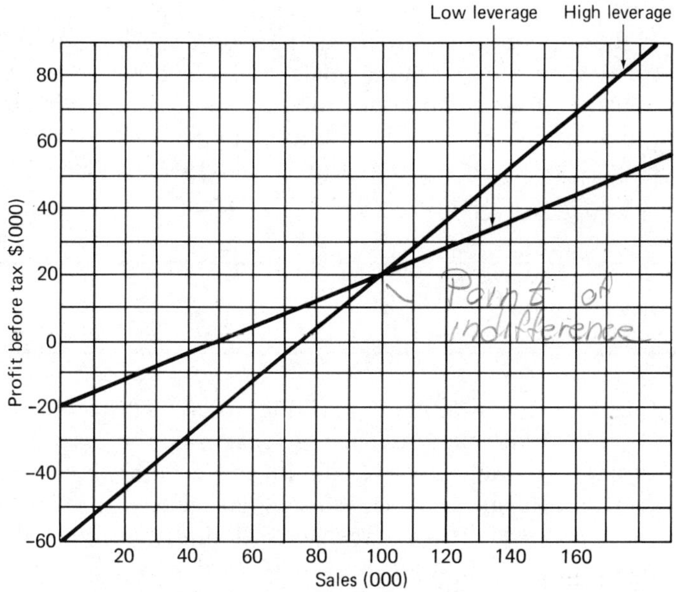

Figure 4–3 Indifference chart

The indifference chart is prepared by identifying the profit before tax at two levels of sales for each production method and then drawing a line through these two points. In this case, we had already computed the profit before tax for both production methods at $100,000 of sales in Table 4–1. From that table, we can also easily see that the loss at a zero sales level will be equal to fixed costs: $20,000 with the low-leverage option and $60,000 with the high-leverage option.

Indifference charts are frequently used for pricing and promotion strategy. For example, a manufacturer of microcomputers faces a choice between two basic marketing strategies. His first alternative is attempting to sell his microcomputers directly to businesses. To sell directly, he must use a commission sales force and a relatively high price, thereby counting on lower fixed marketing costs, higher prices, and higher profit margins per unit. Alternately, the manufacturer can attempt to sell in the much larger individual market by developing a dealer network, advertising extensively, and charging a lower price. The profit potential from the mass market strategy is much greater. However, this strategy causes the break-even point to rise dramatically because fixed costs rise and profit margins decline. Choosing the wrong strategy can lead to bankruptcy.

In many lines of business, a strategy that attempts to capture the best of both alternatives is used. Companies begin by selling a higher-priced unit aimed at a limited market for the purpose of recovering development costs and reaching an early break-even point. Following this, they modify the equipment slightly and bring out a version priced and promoted for the mass market. The break-even point in the mass market is then lower because initial development costs have already been recovered.

Conclusion

Profitability is a major driving force behind most enterprises, whether or not they see their goal as making a profit. Profit is seldom achieved by accident; it is achieved by managers who constantly work to allocate and use resources efficiently. In this chapter, two of the most widely used methods of profitability analysis—earning power analysis and break-even analysis—have been illustrated. Use of these techniques can help managers to identify factors affecting profitability and to plan for greater profitability in the future.

Solved problems

Problem 1 Bestway Electric Appliances has been experiencing declining profitability. Use the earning power system to identify problem areas. Industry averages for use in making comparisons appear with the correct ratio calculations in the solution.

Bestway Electric Appliances

Balance sheets for:					
	Dec. 31 1981	*Dec. 31 1982*		*Dec. 31 1981*	*Dec. 31 1982*
Cash	$ 80,000	$ 90,000	Accounts payable	$ 50,000	$ 55,000
Accounts receivable	170,000	190,000	Notes payable	110,000	135,000
Inventory	200,000	220,000	Total current liabilities	160,000	190,000
Total current assets	450,000	500,000			
Fixed assets (net)	200,000	220,000	Long-term debt	90,000	105,000
Total assets	$650,000	$720,000	Stockholders' equity		
			Common stock ($1 par)	100,000	100,000

(*cont.*)

Balance Sheets for:

Dec. 31 1981	Dec. 31 1982		Dec. 31 1981	Dec. 31 1982
		Paid-in capital	100,000	100,000
		Retained earnings	200,000	225,000
		Total shareholders equity	400,000	425,000
		Total liabilities and net worth	$650,000	$720,000

Income statements for years ending:

		Dec. 31 1981		Dec. 31 1982
Sales		$900,000		$1,000,000
Cost of goods sold	$720,000		$808,000	
General & admin. exp.	80,000		90,000	
Depreciation	20,000		22,000	
Total operating exp.		820,000		920,000
Operating profit		80,000		80,000
Interest		13,000		17,000
Earnings before taxes		67,000		63,000
Taxes		26,000		24,000
Net profit		$ 41,000		$ 39,000
Earnings per share		$0.41		$0.39

Solution The correct ratios are as follows:

	1981	*1982*	*Industry average*
Activity ratios			
Days' receivables outstanding	69 days	69 days	57 days
Inventory turnover	N/A	3.8	3.8
Total asset turnover	1.4	1.4	1.4
Profitability ratios			
Net profit margin	4.6%	3.9%	4.9%
Net return on assets	6.3%	5.4%	6.9%
Operating profit margin	8.9%	8.0%	9.3%
Operating return on assets	12.3%	11.1%	13.0%
Return on net worth	10.3%	9.2%	13.0%

Return on net worth was below the industry average in 1977 and fell further in 1978. A similar pattern was observed for all profitability ratios. The cause can be pursued using the relationship

$$\text{operating return on assets} = \text{operating profit margin} \times \text{total asset* turnover}$$

$$
\begin{aligned}
1977\text{:}\quad 12.3\% &= 8.9\% \times 1.4 \\
1978\text{:}\quad 11.1\% &= 8.0\% \times 1.4 \\
\text{Industry:}\quad 13.0\% &= 9.3\% \times 1.4
\end{aligned}
$$

Asset turnover has remained at the same level as the rest of the industry. The problem lies in the factors affecting profit margin. Operating expenses have risen at a faster rate than sales.

Problem 2 Luing, president of Luing Products, was reviewing the performance of the company's boat division, Abbott Boats. Abbott Boats became a subsidiary of Luing Products several years earlier when controlling interest was acquired from its founder, Jerry Abbott. While sales had increased, the division had still not reached a satisfactory profit level, and Luing was considering an attempt to sell the division. Assets committed to the operation totaled $500,000, and, within fairly broad ranges, changes in sales would not result in changes in assets committed. The average boat was sold at a wholesale price of $2,500 and variable costs per boat averaged $2,000. Fixed operating costs were $200,000 per year. Five hundred boats were sold last year, producing a net operating income of $50,000 and an operating return on assets (net operating income ÷ assets committed) of 10 percent. Luing products requires an operating return on assets of 20 percent from all divisions, and Luing indicated that, unless there was strong reason to expect an improvement, plans would be made to sell the boat division.

Abbott was well aware of the low profitability of his division. He was also aware that his position as president of the company he founded would be in serious jeopardy if it were sold. He wanted to prepare an analysis that would convince Luing of the profit potential of the division. Sales of boats in general had been growing at a rate of 10 percent per year, and sales growth at Abbott Boats had been slightly better: 12 percent per year.

a. In order to have a 20 percent operating return on $500,000 of assets committed, the boat division must produce a net operating income of $100,000. Use a break-even chart to deter-

* Rounding leads to small differences.

mine the sales level necessary to achieve this net operating income.

b. At the 12 percent growth rate in sales, how long will it take the boat division to reach this profitability objective?

Solution The break-even chart appears below. From the chart, we can see that revenue of \$1,500,000 is needed to generate net operating income of \$100,000. This is 20 percent greater than the present sales level of \$1,250,000 (\$2,500 × 500). At the present growth rate in sales, this level should be reached in less than two years.

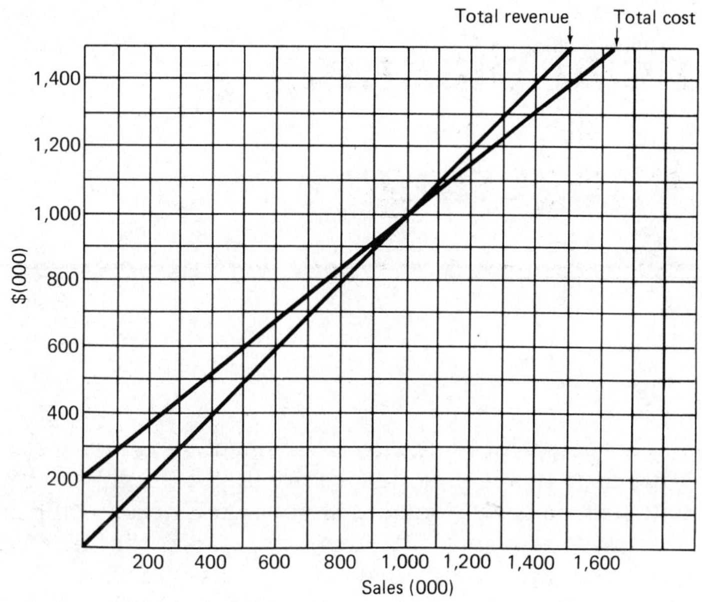

5 Financial planning and budgeting

Some companies seem to lurch from crisis to crisis, always explaining their erratic performance in terms of "unforeseen" events and "uncontrollable" outside factors. And these companies are frequently contrasted with other companies in the industry, companies that produce steady, predictable profits year after year, successful companies that do not seem to be plagued by these same unforeseen circumstances. Although the primary objective of these other, more successful companies, is to lead in profitability, frequently they are industry leaders in size and in growth rates as well. Even within companies, annual reviews reveal inconsistencies—some managers report profitability; others report unforeseen problems. In all probability, unforeseen problems will arise for every manager, but his effectiveness in financial planning and budgeting will help in predicting results and in responding to changing circumstances.

Financial planning is the process of deciding which assets are to be acquired, which expenditures are to be incurred, and where the needed money is to come from. The financial plan must be integrated within the goals and strategy of the firm. The goals and strategy are based on consideration of factors that can be controlled by the firm as well as on projection of conditions in the economy at large. Financial forecasting is a central part of the financial planning process because in selecting the optimum financial plans, the combined impacts of factors that can and cannot be controlled by the company must be considered.

As its name implies, financial forecasting is the process of predicting the future financial structure of the company. Managers use financial forecasting to determine how factors outside of management control, such as economic conditions, will affect financial structure and performance so that they can plan for these conditions in advance. Managers are also interested in the effect of factors within their control on financial structure and performance. For example, a firm may evaluate alternative methods of raising funds by forecasting financial structure and performance under a variety of economic conditions, considering each debt/equity combination.

The typical result of a financial forecast is a set of *pro forma* financial statements: the balance sheet and income statement as they are expected to appear at a particular time, given certain company decisions and external conditions. Financial forecasting consists of three main steps: (1) selection of company decisions and environmental conditions, such as the state of the economy, to be examined; (2) estimation of the impact of each of these variables on the financial structure and performance of the company; and (3) summarization of these results in the form of pro forma financial statements.

Once a financial plan consistent with the firm's goals and objectives has been completed, a series of budgets is prepared. A *budget* is a detailed plan for implementation of a particular part of the overall financial plan. In addition to providing a specific plan of action, the budget serves as a valuable control tool: performance can be compared to the budget on a monthly, weekly, or even daily basis to determine if the financial plan is being followed and to spot any deviations early enough to take corrective action. This chapter begins with the techniques of financial forecasting and concludes with budgeting.

Forecasting financial variables

Pro forma financial statements are the results of many forecasts. The first set of forecasts relates to conditions outside the firm, such as the state of the economy, the availability of raw materials, and the general level of interest rates. Next, a sales forecast for the company is prepared. Because the sales forecast identifies the expected level of activity, most other financial forecasts follow from it. Once the sales and environmental forecasts have been prepared, they are used as the basis for forecasting costs and size of each asset and liability account. Finally, these forecasts are summarized in the form of pro forma financial statements.

As the development of a sales forecast is somewhat beyond the scope of this particular book,[1] this analysis begins with the existence of a sales forecast and covers various ways to forecast individual financial statement variables from the sales forecast.

The forecasting of financial variables depends on the expected behavior of the variables and on the availability of data. Some items, such as rent, advertising, depreciation, and fixed assets, may be known in advance and require no forecasting effort. Other items, such as the level of accounts receivable or the raw material expense, might be expected to remain a constant percentage of sales unless other factors change the relationship. Still other items would be expected to increase with an increase in sales, but not necessarily at the same rate as sales. A certain amount of inventory is required to begin operations, and although inventory increases with the sales level, the amount of inventory needed frequently does not grow as rapidly as the level of sales. Thus, in regard to the impact of sales, there are three types of variables:

a. those that maintain a constant ratio to sales
b. those that are affected by the level of sales, but do not maintain a constant ratio to sales
c. those that are not affected by the level of sales.

Forecasting those things that maintain a constant or near-constant ratio to sales is, of course, quite simple. The sales and accounts receivable levels for Harvey Corporation appear below, along with the ratio of accounts receivable to sales.

Year	*1979*	*1980*	*1981*	*1982*
Sales	1,000	1,100	1,300	1,500
Accounts receivable	161	175	208	240
Accounts receivable / Sales	16.1%	15.9%	16.0%	16.0%

[1] For a good treatment of general forecasting techniques, see William G. Sullivan and W. Wayne Claycombe, *Fundamentals of Forecasting* Reston, Va: Reston Publishing Co. 1977).

Although there were some slight variations, accounts receivable have been stable at approximately 16 percent of sales. Therefore, if 1983 sales are expected to be $1,700, the accounts receivable forecast for 1983 would be $272 ($1,700 × 0.16).

For those items that are not known and are not a constant percentage of sales, the forecasting problem is obviously more difficult. One approach is to use a scatter diagram. Cost of goods sold data for Alrite Corporation appear below and are plotted in Figure 5-1. The company is expecting sales of $130 in 1982 and wishes to forecast the cost of goods sold.

Year	*1978*	*1979*	*1980*	*1981*	*1982*
Sales	$100	$100	$110	$120	$120
Cost of goods sold	60	61	66	70	68

The cost of goods sold is obviously not a constant percentage of sales. As the scatter diagram shows, we cannot fit a straight line without applying some judgement. Based on the scatter diagram, it appears that a cost of goods sold level of approximately $73 would be expected if sales are $130.

Although the approaches to forecasting financial relationships presented here are relatively simple, they are quite useful. More

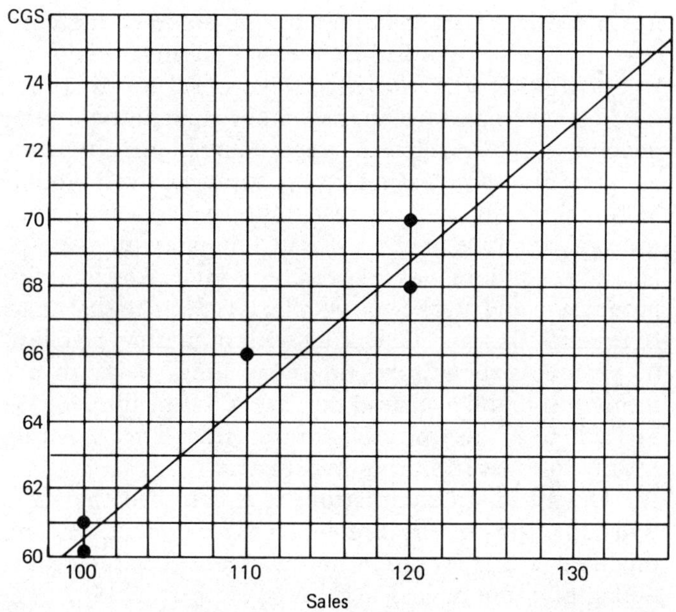

Figure 5-1 Cost of goods sold for Alrite Corporation

advanced methods such as multiple regression and exponential smoothing are available (see footnote, page 60), but no forecasting method is so sophisticated as to eliminate the need for judgement in the development of forecasts. Many considerations, such as the effect of the appointment of a new credit manager, cannot be fit neatly into any purely quantitative forecasting model. The art of successful forecasting lies in the proper balance between those things that can and cannot be quantified.

Pro forma financial statements

Pro forma analysis consists of the preparation of estimated financial statements for future periods. The forecasts of individual financial variables are brought together in the pro forma financial statements.

In preparing pro forma analysis, the normal approach is to start with a sales forecast, move to the income statement, and then on to the balance sheet. Allied Products provides a simple example. The sales forecast for 1982 is $200 million, a substantial increase from the $150 million of sales in 1982. There have been several proposals for the use of the anticipated new profits. Some people are in favor of moving into new areas of business while others want to expand within the company's existing product lines. Still others have argued for increasing dividends or repaying some of the company's long-term debt before it is due. Before making any decisions, management wants to know what the higher level of sales will mean for profitability. Equally important, management must determine if additional financing will be needed to support this higher sales level.

The person preparing the pro forma analysis would begin by projecting the individual expense items that appear on the income statement. According to the 1982 income statement in Table 5–1, the cost of goods sold was 50 percent of sales. After checking with both production and marketing people, it is decided that this ratio is likely to remain constant. Checking with numerous people and adding up of planned expenditures in many areas leads to a projected administrative and overhead expense of $75 million for 1982. As shown in Table 5–1, the projected gross profit and net operating income are readily forecast from this information.

On initial approximation, it is assumed that interest expense will equal the present interest on existing debt. This number can be modified later if the pro forma balance sheet shows that the company will need more or less debt in 1983 than in 1982. The company's

Table 5-1 Allied Products Company

Income statement
(000 omitted)

Year	*1982 (actual)*	*1983 (pro forma)*
Sales	$150,000	$200,000
Cost of goods sold	75,000	100,000
Gross profit	75,000	100,000
Administrative and overhead exp.	60,000	75,000
Net operating income	15,000	25,000
Interest expense	5,000	5,000
Earnings before taxes	10,000	20,000
Income taxes	5,000	10,000
Net income	5,000	10,000
Dividends	2,000	2,100
Increase in retained earnings	3,000	7,900

federal, state and local income taxes have averaged 50 percent of earnings before tax and are expected to continue at this level in the future. Finally, the board of directors has been attempting to follow a policy of steady, modest growth in dividends. Therefore, it is estimated that total dividends will be increased 1 percent to $2.1 million in 1983. This information is used to complete the pro forma income statement, as shown in Table 5-1.

The pro forma income statement was used to project the profit results of operations for a future period while the pro forma balance sheet helps to convert these figures to an estimate of funds needed and available.

Usually the first step in preparing a pro forma balance sheet is the examination of the company's working capital position. The amount of inventory needed and accounts receivable generated are directly related to sales. Likewise, the accounts payable and accruals outstanding are directly related to company expenditures, which are directly related to sales. An analysis of the historical relationship between working capital and sales at Allied Products has revealed a steady relationship: current assets have averaged 80 percent of sales and current liabilities have averaged 20 percent of sales. Discussions with marketing and inventory managers have led to the conclusion that these relationships will remain stable. Consequently, current assets of $160 million (0.80 × $200 million) and current liabilities of

Table 5-2 Allied Products Company

	Balance sheets (000 omitted)	
December 31,	*1982 (actual)*	*1983 (pro forma)*
Current assets	$120,000	$160,000
Fixed assets (net of depreciation)	80,000	100,000
Total assets	$200,000	$260,000
Current liabilities	$ 30,000	$ 40,000
Long-term debt (10%)	50,000	50,000
Common stock	40,000	40,000
Retained earnings	80,000	87,900
Total liabilities and net worth	$200,000	$217,900
Funds needed		$ 42,100

$40 million (0.2 × $200 million) were used in the preparation of the pro forma balance sheet in Table 5-2.

Generally, the level of fixed assets one year ahead can be estimated by looking at current capital budgeting plans and existing depreciation schedules. It is estimated that 1983 depreciation will be $10 million and the company will acquire new fixed assets at a cost of $30 million. Thus, fixed assets at the end of 1983 are expected to be:

1983 fixed assets (in millions) = $80 − $10 + $30 = $100

Based on this, the asset side of the balance sheet was completed.

To complete the liability and net worth portion of the balance sheet, it is tentatively assumed that the company will not issue new debt or common stock. Thus, long-term debt remains at $50 million and common stock remains at $40 million. Retained earnings will increase by the projected increase in retained earnings on the pro forma income statement:

1983 retained earnings (in millions) = $80 + $7.9 = $87.9

The projected total assets are $220 million while the projected total liabilities and net worth are $217.9 million. The $42.1 million excess of projected total assets over projected total liabilities and net worth means that projected funding will *not* be sufficient to meet the projected total asset needs. Allied Products will need $42.1 billion in additional funding to meet 1983 projected needs. This need can be met by borrowing, selling additional stock, or acquiring fewer assets.

Pro forma analysis is a valuable tool for many financial planning purposes. Someone starting a new company uses pro forma analysis in evaluating potential profitability and risk as well as in planning for needed financing. For an existing company, pro forma analysis is used not only in developing plans for the upcoming year but also in evaluating possible new lines of business. It is particularly useful for looking at how one activity will affect the company as opposed to just looking at that activity in isolation.

Pro forma analysis is used frequently for "what if" analysis: "What will our financial position be if . . . . ?" Therefore, many sets of pro forma statements will represent situations managers hope will not occur. A company trying to decide whether to finance a new project with debt may want pro forma analysis under the assumption that when debt is used a recession follows. This allows managers to measure the likely impact of a recession and determine if the additional debt would force the company into default if a recession occurred. With this type of analysis, the company can determine how much money it can safely borrow.

Another set of pro forma statements can represent the financial statement top management expects to see at the end of the year. This set becomes the overall company plan. It is interpreted and implemented through a set of budgets which, if followed, will help to coordinate activities throughout the company for the achievement of the firm's objectives.

Budgets

The functions of a manager are frequently described as planning, organizing, and controlling. Just as pro forma statements are major planning tools, budgets are powerful tools for organizing and controlling. Budgets provide the guidance necessary if the efforts of the various managers are to be coordinated in the pursuit of the profitability objective.

Budgets aid in control by providing standards to use in monitoring performance. At frequent intervals—at least monthly for most firms and as often as daily for some—each area of the business is evaluated in comparison with the budget. Deviations from the plan can be dealt with as quickly as possible by taking corrective action or by modifying the plan. Prompt recognition of deviations gives managers the opportunity to take corrective action before the company's financial position has been allowed to deteriorate.

A well-organized company will have budgets covering many different levels of operations. The entire marketing department will have a sales budget while each individual sales representative will have a quota representing his/her part of the overall budget. The marketing department will also have expense budgets on an overall and an individual level. Likewise, the company will have production budgets, personnel budgets, supply budgets, insurance budgets, etc. Each budget serves to coordinate the activities of a certain area with the overall objectives of the organization.

Flexible budgets. Even the most careful financial planning and budgeting program will not completely relieve the company of the necessity to deal with change. The flexible budget is a tool that has the advantage of allowing for changes in the environment while still providing guidelines for performance. The most widely used type of flexible budget is the budget that changes with the level of sales or production. Obviously, it would make more sense to state the raw materials budget in terms of cost per unit produced rather than in terms of a total dollar figure independent of the amount produced. More subtly, items such as administrative expense also vary with the level of production, but will almost certainly rise without limit under the umbrella of increased production if some method of control is not exercised. The flexible budget can also be used in areas like this to allow flexibility while still providing standards for performance and control.

Use of budgets. If managers are to use budgeting techniques successfully, certain guidelines must be kept in mind. First, a budget is a tool to be used in achieving the firm's objectives; it is not the objective. Improperly designed budgets linked with reward and punishment systems can lead to activity opposite from that desired by the company. There are many examples of maintenance budgets that have led to managers being rewarded for *not* performing maintenance. Similarly, the rewards associated with meeting many sales budgets lead to sales people spending the last two days of every month trying to shift sales from one month to the next rather than selling the product. If a budget is not carefully designed to encourage the desired activity, it can be worse than no budget at all.

Second, budgets must be realistic. This writer was once called in as a consultant because certain divisions of a company constantly failed to perform according to budget. These divisions suffered from low morale and high turnover of managers. The company set all of its budgets according to the standard of one division that happened to be in a unique, highly profitable, market situation. When managers of other divisions failed to meet their budgets, top management either reduced their salary or dismissed them, but made no effort to find out why they were not performing according to budget. When division managers realized that their budgets were unattainable, they quit trying and began concentrating their efforts on finding new employment. Unrealistic high standards can result in decreased profitability.

Cash budgets

A budget of particular interest for financial planning is the cash budget. It is a summary of all projected cash flows for a period of time. The cash budget is usually prepared for a relatively limited time period, such as a year, and is normally broken down into subperiods. A common approach is to prepare a cash budget month by month for the next year. The normal starting point for such a budget is the sales forecast broken down to monthly sales. From the sales forecast it is possible to estimate collections of accounts receivable, payment for inventory, and other cash payments. The cash budget deals only with cash and ignores items such as depreciation expense.

Powell Wholesale Supply provides an example. The company wishes to plan for its cash flow for the first six months of 1983. The completed cash budget appears in Table 5-3. The steps in preparing it are discussed in the following paragraphs.

The first step in preparing the cash budget is the development of a monthly sales forecast. This is done by studying past seasonal patterns and using this information to break the annual sales forecast down into monthly sales.

Few companies make all of their sales on a cash basis; most extend credit to at least some of their customers. Cash comes in from *cash* sales and from the collection of accounts receivable. In the case of Powell Wholesale, all sales are on one-month credit terms with payment due in the month following sales. However, an average of 20 percent of payments are late, being paid two months following the sale. For example, total projected cash inflow for March is 80 percent of February sales plus 20 percent of January sales.

The second step is to identify the cash outflows. The company has a cost of goods sold equal to 50 percent of sales, and goods are pur-

Table 5–3 Powell Wholesale Supply

Cash budget for the first six months of 1983

	Nov.	*Dec.*	*Jan.*	*Feb.*	*Mar.*	*Apr.*	*May*	*June*	*July*
Sales	$20,000	$20,000	$30,000	$30,000	$40,000	$50,000	$40,000	$30,000	$20,000
Collection of 80% of previous month's sales			16,000	24,000	24,000	32,000	40,000	32,000	
Collection of 20% of sales two months earlier			4,000	4,000	6,000	6,000	8,000	10,000	
Total cash receipts			20,000	28,000	30,000	38,000	48,000	42,000	
Payment for inventory			15,000	20,000	25,000	20,000	15,000	10,000	
Wages			10,000	10,000	10,000	10,000	10,000	10,000	
Rent			1,500	1,500	1,500	1,500	1,500	1,500	
Utilities			500	500	500	500	500	500	
Lease payment				2,000		2,000		2,000	
Total cash outflow			27,000	34,000	37,000	34,000	27,000	24,000	
Net cash flows			(7,000)	(6,000)	(7,000)	4,000	21,000	18,000	
Beginning cash			15,000	8,000	8,000	8,000	8,000	20,000	
Unadjusted balance			8,000	2,000	1,000	12,000	29,000	38,000	
Borrow (repay)			0	6,000	7,000	(4,000)	(9,000)	0	
Cumulative borrowing				$ 6,000	$13,000	$ 9,000	0	0	

chased for cash one month in advance of sales. For example, December inventory purchases were 0.50 × $30,000 = $15,000.

In addition to purchase of inventory, Powell has certain other expenses. First of all the company pays wages of $10,000 per month, rent of $1,500 per month, and utilities of $500 per month. In addition, Powell must make lease payments of $2,000 which are due in February, April, and June. These various items are then added up to give total payments for each month.

Having completed the collections of accounts receivable (the only form of cash inflow in this case) and the total payments, the third step is to find the net cash flow for each month. This is, of course, simply the difference between inflows and outflows.

The last step is to project the short-term borrowing needs and repayment schedules. The company had a cash balance of $15,000 on December 31 and wants to maintain a minimum cash balance of $8,000. The net cash flow for the month is added to the beginning cash balance for the month. The result is the unadjusted cash balance, which is the amount of cash the company will have at the end of the month if it neither borrows or repays debt during the month. The borrow (repay) line is the amount that will be borrowed or repaid each month in order to owe as little as possible and still maintain a cash balance of at least $8,000.

The peak borrowing need is reached in March, and the company expects to begin paying the loan back in April, completing payment in May. Since the borrowing needs appear to be temporary, the company should have little difficulty arranging financing if it is in sound financial shape otherwise. Lenders will consider the company a better risk if needs are recognized in advance and if management can benefit from planning ahead for funds needs.

The cash budget is also a useful control tool. Actual cash flows can be compared to the budget for each period and any deviation can be dealt with quickly before the situation gets out of hand. Other budgets, such as the sales, production and advertising budgets, are also used as guides for action and as standards for evaluating performance.

Conclusion

To survive and continue to attract resources, every organization must demonstrate an ability to use resources efficiently. Profitability is a way to measure the efficiency of resource usage. Financial planning and budgeting are the means by which resources are used effectively. Therefore, financial planning and budgeting are important whether or not a profit (in the traditional sense) is being sought and whether or not the firm is currently profitable.

Objectives aren't met without a plan. And plans are never realized without constant monitoring and follow up. In this section, we have covered some of the methods used for developing financial plans and some of the budgeting methods used to implement and to follow up on these plans. Improperly used, these methods can increase the problems of a business. Properly used, they can not only increase profitability and morale, but also decrease risk.

Solved problems

Problem 1 Joyce Brown was employed part-time in a furniture store during her four years of college and has been employed full time with the same store for the two years since graduation. She feels that she has sufficient education in business administration and experience in furniture retailing to consider opening her own store. She has little capital of her own, but she has an uncle who is interested in her plans and may be willing to invest in such an enterprise. As part of her financial planning, she is interested in determining her needs for long-term financing. She has decided that a reasonable approach is to forecast her total assets and current liabilities at the end of one year's operation. The difference between the two must be financed from long-term sources. She expects to just break even on sales of $100,000 during the first year. She intends to lease a store, but fixtures and the like will require a fixed asset investment of $10,000. A minimum cash balance of $5,000 is felt to be prudent. In preparation for her analysis, she referred to *Key Business Ratios* by Dunn and Bradstreet for the following median ratios for furniture stores:

Ratio	*D & B Median*
Average collection period	97 days
Net sales to inventory	4.8
Current ratio	2.76

Forecast net total assets, current liabilities, required long-term financing total liabilities, and net worth.

Brown also wishes to determine what proportion of her long-term financing should be in the form of debt and what portion should be in equity. She again referred to *Key Business Ratios* and noted that the median total debt to net worth ratio for furniture retailers was 96.9 percent.

Solution

Sales (given)	$100,000
Cash (given)	5,000
Accounts receivable (97/365) × $100,000	26,575
Inventory $100,000/4.8	20,833
Total current assets	52,408
Fixed assets (given)	10,000
Total assets	$ 62,408
Current liabilities $52,408/2.76	18,988
Required long-term financing $62,408 − $18,988	$ 43,420
Total liabilities and net worth	$ 62,408

$$\begin{aligned}\text{net worth} + \text{total debt (liabilities)} &= \text{total liabilities and net worth}\\ \text{net worth} + 0.969 \times \text{net worth} &= \$62{,}408\\ 1.969 \times \text{net worth} &= \$62{,}408\\ \text{net worth} &= \$31{,}695\end{aligned}$$

$$\begin{aligned}\text{total debt} &= \$62{,}408 - \$31{,}695 = 30{,}713\\ \text{long-term debt} &= \text{total debt} - \text{current liabilities}\\ \text{long-term debt} &= \$30{,}713 - \$18{,}988 = \$11{,}725\end{aligned}$$

The right side of the balance sheet should then appear as follows:

Current liabilities	$18,988
Long-term debt	11,725
Owners' equity	31,695
Total liabilities and net worth	$62,408

Problem 2 Gold Coast Manufacturing collects receivables on terms of net 60. Purchases of inventory each month equal 50 percent of the next month's expected sales. Inventory is paid for during the month following purchase. Labor expense equals $2 per month, regardless of the sales level.

A tax payment of $1 is expected in March, and a sinking fund payment of $5 is due in March. Selling and administrative expenses will average $1 per month. A plant modernization payment of $10 is due in January. An interest payment of $1 is due in March. The January 1 cash balance is $5, and there is no short-term debt. The minimum cash balance is $5. The company will borrow short term against its line of credit to maintain this cash balance. Sales for the last months of 1978 and projected sales for the first half of 1979 appear next. Prepare a cash budget for the first six months of 1979.

Month	*Sales*
November	$12
December	13
January	10
February	10
March	10
April	10
May	8
June	8
July	8

Solution

	Nov.	*Dec.*	*Jan.*	*Feb.*	*Mar.*	*Apr.*	*May*	*June*
Monthly sales	$12	$13	$10	$10	$10	$10	$ 8	$ 8
Collection AR			12	13	10	10	10	10
Inventory purchases		5	5	5	5	4	4	
Payment accounts payable			5	5	5	5	4	4
Direct labor			2	2	2	2	2	2
Tax payment					1			
Sinking fund payment					5			
Selling and admin. exp.			1	1	1	1	1	1
Plant modernization			10					
Interest payment					1			
Total payments			18	8	15	8	7	7
Net cash flow			(6)	5	(5)	2	3	3
Beginning cash			5	5	5	5	5	5
Unadjusted cash balance			(1)	10	0	7	8	8
Borrow (repay)			6	(5)	5	(2)	(3)	(1)
Ending cash balance		$ 5	$ 5	$ 5	$ 5	$ 5	$ 5	$ 7
Cumulative borrowing		$ 0	$ 6	$ 1	$ 6	$ 4	$ 1	$ 0

Problem 3 Refer to the financial statements for Office Supply Corporation presented in Chapter 3. Office Supply wishes to prepare pro forma financial statements for 1983. A sales forecast of $140 has been prepared. The company has no plans for additional borrowing, debt repayment, stock issue, or stock retirement at this time. All net income will be paid out in the form of dividends. A compensating balance requirement sets minimum cash needs at $10. A new credit manager has been hired, and he feels that he can increase accounts receivable turnover to 4 by the end of the year without losing sales. An investigation of changes in inventory reveals that the decreased turnover in 1982 was caused by expansion of product lines. They estimate that, in addition to the existing stock, inventory equal to 20 percent of any sales over $120 will be required. Fixed asset turnover is expected to follow the trend of the last several years. Sales for 1977, 1978, and 1979 were $60, $70, and $75, respectively. Current liabilities for 1977, 1978, and 1979 were $15, $18, and $20, respectively. Office Supply's operating expenses for 1977, 1978, and 1979 were $18, $21, and $22.50, respectively. Graph space is provided for your use in preparing forecasts.

Solution Office Supply Corporation

Pro forma income statement
year ending December 31, 1983

Sales	$140
Cost of goods sold	70
Gross profit	70
Administrative and overhead expenses	42
Net operating income	28
Interest	6
Earnings before taxes	22
Taxes	11
Net income	$ 11

Pro forma balance sheet
December 31, 1983

Assets		*Liabilities and net worth*	
Cash	$ 10	Accounts payable	$ 25
Accounts receivable	35	Miscellaneous accruals	25
Inventory	34	Total current liabilities	50
Current assets	79	Long-term debt	60
Fixed assets	70	Common stock	10
Total assets	$149	Paid-in capital	10
		Retained earnings	30
		Total liabilities and net worth	$160
			($ 11)

The following analysis was used in preparing this answer:

Year	*1977*	*1978*	*1979*	*1980*	*1981*	*1982*
Sales	$60	$70	$75	$80	$100	$120
Admin. and op. exp ÷ sales	0.30	0.30	0.30	0.31	0.30	0.30
Current liabilities ÷ sales	0.25	0.257	0.267	0.25	0.30	0.333
Cost of goods sold ÷ sales				0.50	0.50	0.50
Fixed assets ÷ sales				0.50	0.50	0.50

Interest: Based on statement that no change in debt is expected

Cash: Based on $10 compensating balance requirement

Accounts receivable: $140 ÷ 4 = $35

Inventory: $30 + 0.20($140 − $120) = $34

Fixed assets: 0.50 × $140 = $70

Total current liabilities: This is the most difficult item to forecast in this problem, and no two people are expected to get exactly the same answer.

The $50 estimate is based on the observed trend in current liabilities ÷ sales over recent years. A ratio of 0.35 or 0.36 seems reasonable for 1983. Fifty dollars is about midway between these two.

6
Working capital management

Working capital management includes the management of both current assets and current liabilities. It is important because current assets represent over half of the assets of the typical business and current liabilities represent a major claim against the company's cash flows. As current assets represent a major portion of the company's assets, managers must invest in only those current assets that will make contributions to profitability. Likewise, care is required in managing current liabilities so that payments can be made when they fall due.

The term *working capital* means total current assets, the primary current assets being cash, marketable securities, accounts receivable, and inventory. Although these assets are not productive in the same sense that a manufacturing plant is productive, they do contribute to profitability in that they are essential for the operation of the business. Careful management is necessary for keeping current assets at the level that maximizes profitability.

The primary current liabilities are accounts payable, accrued liabilities, and loans that are due within one year. Many current liabilities are cost-free in the sense that no direct interest payment is made. Furthermore, the interest rate on short-term debt is sometimes lower than for long-term debt. However, current liabilities require cash payment within a short time, and, thereby, jeopardize a company's ability to meet obligations in an economic downturn. The goal of current liability management is to select a mix of current liabilities and a total level of current liabilities that achieves a satisfactory trade off between cost and risk.

Cash management

Cash, including both currency and checking account balances, is used for day-to-day transactions. Cash is constantly being used to meet current obligations and is constantly being replenished from the sale of inventory or services and from the collection of accounts receivable. Some reserve cash must be maintained as inflows do not necessarily equal outflows on any given day.

Two types of costs are associated with cash reserves. Idle cash does not earn a return, and even if the reserve cash is temporarily invested in low-risk securities, the returns are frequently low. This foregone return is the first type of cost. The other costs are associated with the risk of running out of cash and extend from the relatively mild costs of additional borrowing to the more drastic costs of forced sale of assets. Large cash reserves minimize the likelihood of the second type of costs while small cash reserves minimize the first type. Managers attempt to keep idle cash at the lowest possible level without jeopardizing ability to meet current obligations.

A number of things can be done to minimize the amount of reserve cash needed. First of all, cash budgeting can be used to predict cash flows accurately, and thereby decrease the reserves needed. Secondly, maintenance of credit arrangements such as bank lines of credit allows the company to borrow quickly and economically in the event of a temporary cash shortage, which reduces the amount of excess cash needed.

In addition, efficient cash management methods can minimize the amount of idle cash needed. A lock-box system is one such method. With a lock-box system, a company instructs customers to mail their checks to regional post office box numbers rather than to its home office. Banks at each location pick up checks from the post office several times a day and deposit them immediately. Payments are credited to the company's bank balance immediately and are credited to the customers' accounts when the reports reach the home office. This system often frees up millions of dollars otherwise tied up in the mail or in processing.

As an example of the profitability potential of efficient cash management, consider a medium sized insurance company that receives $2 million a day in premiums. Previously checks were mailed to the home office, requiring an average of two days in the mail, and were then processed, requiring one additional day, before being deposited in the bank. Thus, the company constantly had three days' premiums—$6 million—either in the mail or in processing. The company decided to change to a lock box system, thus reducing mailing time to one day and predeposit processing time to zero days. This system reduced funds in the mail and in processing from $6 million to $2 million, freeing up $4 million. If the lock box system costs $100,000 per year to operate, the freed up money costs 2.5 percent (100,000/4,000,000). At present interest rates, this represents a very inexpensive way to acquire additional money to invest.

Concentration banking is another method used to reduce idle cash. If a company writes checks from a dozen different accounts, it must keep sufficient funds to allow for fluctuations in each of those accounts. This need can be reduced by writing all of the company's checks from a single bank. If a lock-box system is used for collection, the money can be transferred into this one account by wire transfer every day.

Marketable securities

Financial managers of larger companies adjust their cash balances every day, either investing temporarily or borrowing so that the days' end checking account balance is as close to zero as possible. Five million dollars invested for *one day* at a 15 percent annual interest rate results in interest income of over two thousand dollars. Thus, it is obviously worthwhile for corporations with large daily cash flows to make these kinds of daily adjustments. Through bank cash management services and money market mutual funds, opportunities to profitably use temporarily idle money have become available to many smaller firms as well.

In addition to funds that are idle for only a day or two, many companies experience seasonal cycles in operations of such magnitude that they have idle money during part of the year and must borrow at other times. Under those circumstances, many companies find themselves in the position of holding money for some specific future need or as a reserve for possible unforseen liquidity needs. Profitability can be increased by investing these funds as profitably as possible.

A number of approaches to temporary investment are available. One such approach has recently become available and is a service provided by banks themselves. For a fee, the bank will monitor the firm's account on a daily basis, transferring money to and from interest bearing accounts or portfolios of short-term, low-risk investments. As an alternative, a company may use one of the many money-market mutual funds that are available, moving money back and forth between the fund and the bank as needed. Because money can be transferred to and from these money-market funds by wire transfer, there is no delay in meeting a demand for funds.

Larger companies frequently prefer to invest directly in money-market instruments on a daily basis and smaller companies may prefer direct investment when funds are going to be idle for a few weeks or a few months. Direct investment is not subject to the fees associated with other management services. By definition, a money market instrument has a maturity of less than one year, is very safe, and can be resold quickly. Some of the major money-market instruments purchased for this purpose are:

U.S. Treasury bills—obligations of the United States government with maturities of 91 to 182 days.

Repurchase agreements—a form of loan to a U.S. government security dealer to help him finance his inventory of securities. The maturity of these loans is frequently as short as one day.

Negotiable certificates of deposits—bank obligations with varying maturities. They differ from other certificates of deposit in that there is a market in which they can be sold to other investors if the company experiences an unexpected need for funds.

Inventory management

The level of investment in inventory affects total assets and, therefore, operating return on assets. It also affects sales since decreased inventory levels increase the probability of stock-outs and of lost sales. The objective of inventory management is to minimize total inventory costs, consisting of ordering costs, carrying costs, and lost sales opportunity costs. The two major inventory decisions are the reorder point—the inventory level at which a new order is placed—and the reorder quantity, which is the quantity ordered each time.

As the reorder quantity increases, carrying costs increase and ordering costs decrease. The goal, then, is to select a reorder quantity that minimizes the sum of these costs. The reorder quantity that achieves this minimum cost is found by the formula:

$$ROQ = \sqrt{(2 \times S \times O)/C}$$

S is total demand per year, O is the cost associated with placing an order, and C is the cost of carrying an item in inventory for a year. The cost of placing an order is primarily an administrative expense. The cost of carrying inventory includes the cost of funds tied up as well as warehousing expenses.

For example, ABC Corporation sells 50,000 units of its product per year. Ordering costs are \$100 per order, and carrying costs are \$10 per unit per year. The optimal reorder quantity is:

$$ROQ = \sqrt{(2 \times 50{,}000 \times 100)/10} = \sqrt{1{,}000{,}000} = 1{,}000 \text{ units}$$

The *reorder point*—the inventory level at which a new order is placed—affects both the lost sales opportunity cost and the inventory carrying cost. As the reorder point increases, the probability of lost sales due to lack of inventory decreases. However, it does not go to zero. Figure 6–1 shows a typical distribution of demand for a product. As inventory levels are continually raised, the increase in carrying costs is offset with less and less decrease in the probability of a stock-out. The objective in establishing a reorder point policy is to make the trade off between inventory carrying cost and lost sales opportunity cost that maximizes profitability.

The problem involved can be illustrated with the simplified example of Southern Technical Corporation. Southern loses \$1 in profit every time it is unable to fill an order for lack of inventory. The demand for the company's product is 100 units during half of the months and 200 units during the other months. However, there is no way to know in advance whether the demand for a particular month will be 100 or 200 units. An optimum reorder quantity of 150 units has been determined, so an order is placed an average of once a month. It takes one month for a shipment to arrive at Southern once it has been ordered. If Southern orders every time inventory reaches 100 units, it will have enough inventory to meet demand during half

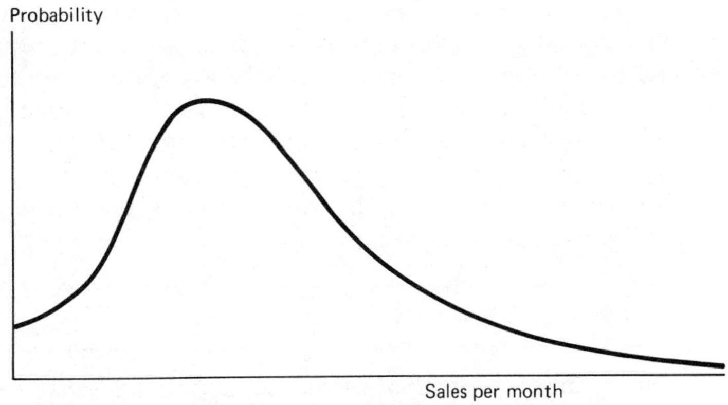

Figure 6-1 Typical demand distribution

of the months, but will lose sales of 100 units during the other half. Thus, the average monthly lost sales cost will be $50 at a reorder point of 100 units. The cost accountants have determined that carrying costs will be $50 per month at this reorder point, so the total of these two costs is $100.

The sales manager is pressing for a 200 unit reorder point so that lost sales can be eliminated. The cost accountants have estimated that monthly carrying cost would be $125 at this reorder point. Therefore, while the lost sales cost would be zero, the carrying cost would exceed the sum of lost sales cost and of carrying cost at the 100 unit reorder point.

The above example is an oversimplification in that very few companies will experience only two possible levels of demand. Furthermore, the time between order and receipt is also subject to uncertainty. The procedure for analysis would be the same if there were hundreds of different possible levels of demand, but the analysis would be done using computer simulation because the computations would be much too tedious to perform otherwise. Smaller and less sophisticated companies frequently rely on judgement and experience as the alternative to computer analysis.

Accounts receivable management

Generous credit policy can result in increased sales. Offsetting factors include the cost of money tied up in accounts receivable and increased risk of bad debt loss. The objective of accounts receivable management is to make the trade off that maximizes profitability. Of paramount importance is deciding to whom credit should be granted. In making this decision, the company must decide how to evaluate potential credit customers and how to decide which potential customers should be granted credit. Second, the company must choose the terms: credit period and prompt payment discount. A third policy area deals with monitoring accounts receivable and collecting delinquent accounts.

Credit evaluation

Ideally, the credit evaluation would allow the company to classify all potential customers as to whether or not they will subsequently default. Of course, this is impossible. Therefore, what can be done is to identify those who are and those who are not likely to default.

The primary considerations in any credit analysis are commonly referred to as the three Cs of credit: character, capacity, and collateral.

Character deals with the potential credit customer's willingness to pay his obligations. Character of both firms and individuals is evaluated primarily by questioning other firms from whom they have borrowed in the past. For a new company with no past borrowing experience, the past credit behavior of the senior managers will be of interest.

Capacity has to do with the ability to repay a loan: does the potential customer have enough income or cash flow to make the required payments? For individuals, credit grantors have developed rules of thumb with regard to an acceptable ratio of income to loan payments. For businesses, times-interest-earned and fixed charge coverage provide measures of capacity. For instance, a company might have a policy of not providing credit unless the customer had a times-interest-earned ratio of at least 6.0 and a fixed charge coverage of at least 3.0.

Collateral deals with the question of whether the assets of the potential customer are of sufficient value that they could be sold to repay debts. Collateral is divided between general assets and pledged assets, against which the lender has a specific claim in the event of default. Accounts receivable are seldom backed by a specific pledge; the lender shares a claim against the unpledged assets with other creditors. When a company is forced into bankruptcy, assets are normally sold at a small percentage of their book value. Consequently, a potential creditor would prefer that the ratio of debt-to-total assets be as small as possible. A company might, for example, have a trade credit policy of not extending credit to customers with debt equal to more than 60 percent of the value of their assets. Obviously, the appropriate ratio would vary by industry as risk is greater in some industries than in others.

Using credit agencies in evaluation. When the amount of credit extended is large, the creditor can spend a substantial amount of effort in analyzing the potential customer's credit worthiness. But when the amount involved is small, the decision must be made with minimal time commitment. In either case, the company wants to complete the credit evaluation as quickly and economically as possible. Thus, credit agencies are frequently used. Credit agencies specialize in keeping credit files on companies or on individuals and disseminating the information, for a fee, to companies requesting it. Every community has a credit bureau which keeps files on individual customers, and a single phone call is frequently sufficient to provide all the information necessary for a credit decision on an individual. Dunn and Bradstreet is a national company which provides similar information about businesses. It maintains files on thousands of businesses so that a company can quickly check the credit standing of a potential new customer.

The credit decision

Once all of the credit information has been collected, the potential creditor can either make a subjective judgement or can use some quantitative method to put the potential customer in a credit risk category. For example, Dunn and Bradstreet assigns to each business customer a "grade." Hence, a seller can simply set a particular Dunn and Bradstreet rating as the minimum acceptable standard.

For sales to individuals, credit scoring is frequently used. The individual may be given 1 point for having a telephone, 2 points for living at the same address for more than three years, 2 points for being employed by the same employer for more than three years, etc. If the customer has more points than the minimum required, credit is granted. This approach is widely used by retailers and by loan companies which must have credit decisions made quickly by people without extensive training in credit analysis. The large personal loan companies have statisticians continually trying to refine these scoring formulas so they can grant credit to more people while suffering fewer bad debt losses.

Credit terms

Upon determining who may buy on credit, terms of such credit must be established. Credit terms include the number of days from the invoice date until payment is due and the discount for prompt payment, if any. Credit terms are stated in abbreviated form such as: 2/10, net 30. These particular terms mean that the buyer is required to pay within 30 days of the invoice date, and receives a 2 percent discount if payment is made within 10 days. This same notation is used with variations in due date, discount, and number of days to take advantage of the discount. Some other standard forms of credit terminology are:

C.O.D.—cash on delivery

C.B.D.—cash before delivery

E.O.M.—payment is due at the end of the month following sale.

Seasonal dating—extended credit terms encouraging retailers to accept inventory early, thereby relieving the manufacturer of shipping problems. For example, a textbook publisher might treat all sales made during the summer as if they were made on September 1.

Normally the discount makes it rather expensive to wait until the due date to pay the bill. For example, a customer who buys $100 worth of goods on terms of 2/10, net 30, pays only $98 if payment is made by the tenth day. To wait until the thirtieth day, the customer must pay the full $100, or a 2.04 percent (2/98) fee for the use of the money from the tenth to the thirtieth day. Paying 2.04 percent for the use of the money for twenty days is equivalent to an annual interest rate of:

$$\frac{2}{98} \times \frac{365}{30 - 10} = 0.0204 \times 18.25 = 37.2\%$$

From the seller's point of view, longer credit terms mean that more funds are tied up in accounts receivable. The question is whether the increased sales justify the increased funds tied up. Many companies that sell to other companies try to set credit terms so that the receivables' due date is no greater than the average time inventory is held by the customer. Credit terms serve to finance the customer's inventory, but the supplier does not want to provide financing in excess of inventory. Frequently, credit terms are standard in an industry, giving the individual supplier little choice but to offer the same terms.

Monitoring accounts receivable

Regardless of how the credit decisions are originally made, it is important to continually monitor the company's accounts receivable to be sure that credit policy is working. The days' receivables outstanding measure discussed in Chapter 3 provides a quick check on the effectiveness of credit standards and collection policy. The days' receivables outstanding should not be much in excess of that allowed under the company's credit terms, though the days' receivables outstanding is likely to exceed the credit terms by some amount because few customers pay their bills before they are due and some will always be late.

Frequently it is necessary to look beyond the days' receivables outstanding to evaluate the effectiveness of credit standards and of collection policy. If the company has a highly seasonal sales pattern, the days' receivables outstanding will be affected by the date on which the receivables are examined. Additionally, the days' receivables measure is an average and gives no indication of the volume of receivables dangerously past due. Therefore, an aging of receivables provides a more complete picture. Aging consists of classifying all receivables according to their age.

Wright Paper Products is used to demonstrate the usefulness of aging receivables. Wright had sales per year of \$1.5 million in 1981 and 1982. However, receivables climbed from \$237 thousand at the end of 1981 to \$250 thousand at the end of 1982. This, of course, was reflected in an increase in the days' receivables outstanding:

$$\text{1981 days' receivables} = \frac{237{,}000}{2{,}000{,}000} \times 365 = 43 \text{ days}$$

$$\text{1982 days' receivables} = \frac{250{,}000}{2{,}000{,}000} \times 365 = 46 \text{ days}$$

While the increase in days' receivables was modest, the financial vice-president, Thomas Wright, decided to examine the receivables for any early sign of developing difficulty. The accounts receivable information was summarized as presented in Table 6–1.

To enhance the usefulness of this information, it is helpful to state the receivables in some percentage form so they can be compared from year to year. Two methods of aging receivables are shown

Table 6–1 Wright Paper Products

Accounts receivable summary

	1981		*1982*	
	Sales for period	*Sales for period that are still uncollected on December 31*	*Sales for period*	*Sales for period that are still uncollected on December 31*
Dec.	$150,000	$120,000	$200,000	$155,000
Nov.	130,000	65,000	120,000	55,000
Oct.	100,000	20,000	90,000	17,000
Sept.	100,000	12,000	70,000	8,000
Prior to Sept.	1,520,000	20,000	1,520,000	15,000

in Table 6–2. The first set of numbers shows what percentage of receivables outstanding fall in each age category. This widely used approach is fine if the monthly sales pattern has not changed. However, the monthly sales pattern for Wright Paper has obviously changed. Thus, the second set of numbers shows receivables out-

Table 6–2 Wright Paper Products

Aging of accounts receivable as of December 31

As a percentage of total receivables

Percent of receivables	1981	1982
Under 1-month old	50.6%	62.0%
between 1 and 2 months old	27.4	22.0
between 2 and 3 months old	8.4	6.8
between 3 and 4 months old	5.1	3.2
over 4 months old	8.4	6.0

As a percentage of each month's sales

Month	*Percentage of sales from the month still uncollected as of December 31*	
	1981	*1982*
Dec.	80.0%	77.5%
Nov.	50.0	45.8
Oct.	20.0	18.9
Sept.	12.0	11.4
Jan. through Aug.	1.3	1.0

standing from each month as a percentage of sales for that month. By comparing the promptness of payment between periods, this approach makes it possible to overcome seasonal variations. While both approaches are widely used in practice, the second approach is recommended because it is as good as the first if there is no change in the seasonal pattern and is superior if there is a change.

The second aging schedule in Table 6-2 should be used in this case because the monthly sales pattern has changed. The aging reveals that the collection of receivables has actually improved. The percentage of receivables outstanding from each previous month has actually declined. The apparent slowdown suggested by the accounts receivable turnover resulted from a change in the monthly sales pattern.

Current liabilities

Current liabilities are obligations that fall due within one year. A firm must decide what portion of assets should be financed through short-term sources, what particular short-term sources should be used, and the interaction between current assets and current liabilities. In the following paragraphs, this interaction is stressed. A more extensive discussion of sources of short-term financing is in Chapter 11.

The three main types of current liabilities are accrued liabilities, accounts payable, and short-term loans. A firm will always want to make maximum use of accrued liabilities and accounts payable, up to the point where valuable discounts must be passed up, because these are essentially cost-free sources of funds. The amount available from these sources can be affected by negotiations with suppliers and by payment policy. While credit terms available are sometimes fixed, there are also many incidents wherein the same supplier is selling to different customers on different credit terms, simply because a number of customers negotiated for the longer terms.

In addition, the use of accrued liabilities and accounts payable can be maximized by maintaining proper payment practices. When a bill arrives, it should not be paid immediately; the date of payment should be set and a filing system should be used so that the bill is then paid on the appropriate date. This allows one to maintain an excellent credit rating while using the suppliers' funds for a reasonable amount of time. It is not uncommon for the financially strongest companies to be among the slowest in payment of bills because they know that suppliers will continue to sell them goods and they can take maximum advantage of cost-free funds to increase their profitability. Of course, the trick is not to extend use of this source to the point where credit rating is affected.

The role of current liabilities in liquidity management. Liquidity refers to the ability to meet cash obligations as they come due, and is one of the major issues involved in working capital management. Current liabilities play an important role in determining liquidity needs. First, the primary reason cash is needed is to pay current liabilities. Second, current liabilities themselves can serve as a source of funds to meet payment needs.

Since the company will want to maximize the use of cost-free funds, the question of the optimal amount of current liabilities normally refers primarily to the optimal amount of short-term debt. When looking at the debt of a firm or individual, the primary issue is capacity: does the borrower have the resources to meet payments? A major disadvantage of short-term debt is that it does fall due quickly, requiring the ability to generate cash from other sources. Balanced against this is the fact that short-term debt is sometimes cheaper than long-term debt and that it gives the company greater flexibility because it can be retired when not needed. Many companies experience seasonal needs for working capital in order to meet peak sales needs. A fairly common practice is to finance these temporary needs with short-term debt each year, while financing the amount that cannot be paid off during some part of each year from permanent sources.

Because funds tied up in cash or short-term investments cannot be working for the firm, they should be kept at the lowest level possible, consistent with maintaining liquidity. Planning for the use of current liabilities as a liquidity source can decrease the need for cash and short-term investment reserves. Lines of credit with banks are one important source of liquidity. A company that maintains a line of credit equal to its estimated seasonal borrowing peak plus a cushion for the unexpected will be in a position to hold minimum balances and rely on borrowing when needed. Accounts payable can also be used as a source in unusual circumstances. In a business downturn or credit crunch, the stretching of payments on accounts payable is a common practice in many industries. Within limits, stretching of payments under these circumstances will reduce the demand for the firm's cash without any serious damage to the credit rating. This source is much more readily available if the company has been scrupulous about paying bills under normal circumstances and informs suppliers *honestly* as to when they can expect payment on late accounts. It does not take a credit manager long to separate those who "cannot understand how their payments got lost in the mail" from those who provide honest information about their financial position.

Conclusion

Working capital management is important to the profitability of the firm because it represents a major use of funds; frequently over half of the firm's total assets are in the form of current assets. Working capital management is also important with regard to risk. For example, poor inventory and accounts receivable management can leave the firm with inventory and accounts receivable that are actually worthless. In addition, working capital management is a major influence on a company's ability to meet demands for cash. Thus, careful working capital planning and control is an important part of profitability and risk management.

Solved problems

Problem 1 American Products has sales of 200,000 units per year. Inventory carrying costs are $50 per year and ordering costs are $500 per order. What is the optimum order quantity?

Solution $\text{ROQ} = \sqrt{(2 \times 200{,}000 \times 500)/50} = \sqrt{4{,}000{,}000} = 2{,}000$ units

Problem 2 Northeast Controls processes orders of 100 units during one-half of the months, 200 units during one quarter of the months, and 300 units during one-quarter of the months. Average inventory carrying costs per month at reorder points of 100, 200, and 300 units are $50, $100, and $175, respectively. Average ordering cost per month is $50 regardless of reorder point. The lost profit per unit of orders lost due to lack of inventory is $2. A reorder point of 100/200/300 will provide the lowest total inventory cost.

Solution

Reorder point	*Order*	*Lost orders*	*Lost order opportunity cost*	*Probability*	*Expected opportunity cost*
	100	0	0	0.50	$ 0
100	200	100	200	0.25	50
	300	200	400	0.25	100
		Total expected opportunity cost =			$150
	100	0	0	0.50	$ 0
200	200	0	0	0.25	0
	300	100	200	0.25	50
					$ 50
	100	0	0	0.50	$ 0
300	200	0	0	0.25	0
	300	0	0	0.25	0
					$ 0

Reorder point	*Expected total inventory cost per month*
100	$50 + $50 + $150 = $250
200	$50 + $100 + $50 = $200
300	$50 + $175 + $0 = $225

The lowest expected total inventory cost per month occurs at a reorder point of 200 units.

Problem 3 Compute the effective interest rate for failure to take advantage of the prompt payment discount under each of the following credit terms:

a. 2/10, net 30

b. 3/30, net 45

c. 3/30, net 90

d. 2/20, net 60

Solution

2/98 × 365/(30 − 10) = 0.0204 × 18.25 = 37.23%
3/97 × 365/(45 − 30) = 0.0309 × 24.33 = 75.18%
3/97 × 365/(90 − 30) = 0.0309 × 6.08 = 18.79%
2/98 × 365/(60 − 20) = 0.0204 × 9.13 = 18.63%

Problem 4 XYZ now sells on terms of net 30 and is considering a change to terms of net 60. XYZ is willing to make all investments with an operating ROA greater than 20 percent. The anticipated effect of the change in credit is summarized as follows:

	Net 30 (actual)	*Net 60 (anticipated)*	*Change*
Sales	$1,000	$1,200	$200
Net operating income	100	120	20
Accounts receivable	82	197	115
Total assets	500	630	130

Solution Operating ROA on the marginal investment equals

$$\frac{\text{change in net operating income}}{\text{change in total assets}} = \frac{20}{130} = 15.4\%$$

They should *not* change to net 60 terms.

7
Time value of money

Virtually every manager is engaged in decision-making which involves the immediate commitment of a sum of money with the expectation of a larger return in the future. Examples are:

> Research and development money is spent today with the hope of increasing profit at a later date.
>
> A sales promotion program requiring acquisition of inventory and purchase of advertising is established with the objective of generating a profit.
>
> People are trained with the expectation that they will produce income for the company in excess of their salaries.
>
> Factories and machines are acquired in anticipation of profits sufficient to justify their original cost.
>
> Money is borrowed with the realization that the amount to be paid back will exceed the amount borrowed.
>
> Investors purchase the company's stock because they believe the stream of dividends they will receive in the future is large enough to justify the present cost of the stock.

Accordingly, to make the most profitable decisions, one must be able to determine the present effective interest rate involved in a payment, in exchange for some series of cash flows expected in the future. One must be able to determine the maximum amount that can be paid for a future payment, if a certain required return is to be earned. Methods of determining these things are covered in this chapter. Those who master this material will improve their ability to make profitable decisions in a wide variety of situations; they will also be able to better understand and work with company budgeting policies, particularly capital budgeting policies.

Concept of compound value

The concept of compounding is fundamental to the analysis of all problems involving payments over time. Assume that Community Bank pays 5 percent interest on savings accounts, with interest compounded annually. A deposit of \$100 will earn \$5 in interest over the next year and, therefore, will grow to \$105 by the end of the year. This form of growth is often written:

$$\$100 \times (1 + 0.05) = \$105$$

If the money is left on deposit for two years, without any interest being withdrawn, interest during the second year will be 5 percent of the \$105 on deposit at the beginning of the second year: $0.05 \times \$105 = \$5.25$. Adding this \$5.25 to the \$105 balance at the end of the first year yields a balance of \$110.25 at the end of the second year. This can be stated in the form of a simple formula:

$$\$105 \times (1 + 0.05) = \$110.25$$

or

$$\$100 \times (1 + 0.05) \times (1.05) = \$110.25$$

or

$$\$100 \times (1.05)^2 = \$110.25$$

The same approach can be used for any number of years. The initial amount is multiplied by 1.05—one time for each year the money is to be left on deposit. As a matter of convenience in writing, the compound value concept can be stated in the simple general formula:

$$FV = PV \times (1 + R)^n$$

in which FV equals the future amount the investor will end up with; PV, the present value; R, the interest rate that will be earned each period; and n, the number of periods the present value will be allowed to grow at interest rate R.

Suppose the \$100 was to be left on deposit in the 5 percent savings account for thirty years. The amount that would be on hand at the end of thirty years is:

$$FV = \$100 \times (1 + 0.05)^{30} = \$432.20$$

The only difficulty in solving this problem is multiplying 1 + 0.05 by itself 30 times. Fortunately, most pocket calculators designed for business use have built-in functions for solving problems of this type. In addition, Table A–1 in the appendix at the end of this book has the completed calculation for several values of R and n, in case a calculator is not handy. The future value of \$432.20 was found by going down the 5 percent column of Table A–1 until the 30-year value of 4.322 was found. 4.322 was then multiplied by \$100 to give the future amount of \$432.20.

Although the idea involved in compound interest is relatively simple, it is also quite powerful. In addition to many uses involving money, the idea is used for such things as population projections and economic growth analyses. It is applicable to any situation wherein growth is a constant percentage of the value at the beginning of each period. Suppose, for example, earnings per share of common stock for a particular company are presently \$4 per share and are growing at a rate of 6 percent per year. How long will it take for earnings to double? The basic compound value can be applied again:

$$FV = PV \times (1 + R)^n$$

$$\$8 = \$4 \times (1 + 0.06)^n$$

or

$$2 = (1.06)^n$$

To find the number of years, it is only necessary to determine the number of years at which $(1.06)^n$ equals or exceeds 2.0. Going down the 6 percent column of Table A–1, 2.012 is found at twelve years. Thus, earnings per share will slightly more than double in twelve years.

The same approach can be used when present and future amounts are known, but the interest rate is unknown. Suppose, for example, an investment costs \$1,000 today and will return \$2,000 in eight years. Using the formula again, the problem is:

$$\$2{,}000 = \$1{,}000 \times (1 + R)^8$$

or

$$2 = (1 + R)^8$$

It is only necessary to go across the eight-year row of Table A–1 until 2.0 is found. 1.851 is found at 8 percent and 2.144 is found at 10 percent. Thus, the return is between 8 percent and 10 percent. Using a calculator with an appropriate function, the return is 9.051 percent per year.

Present value of a future amount

Because money on hand today can be invested to grow to a larger amount in the future, it follows that a dollar promised at some future date is worth less than a dollar on hand today. If an investment promises \$100 a year from today, the alternative to this investment would be a bank account paying 10 percent interest. What would an investor be willing to pay for the promise of \$100 in one year? This question can be answered using the basic compound interest formula:

$$FV = PV(1 + R)^n$$

$$\$100 = PV(1 + 0.10)^2$$

$$PV = \frac{1}{(1 + 0.10)^2} \times \$100 = \$82.64$$

The present value represents the maximum amount one can afford to pay for a future cash flow if a particular rate of return is to be earned. Consequently, the present value is the *value* of the future cash flow to an investor who has alternate opportunities equal to that particular interest rate. If the cost of an investment is below its value, it would be attractive, and vice versa.

The present value analysis above can be generalized for any future time, any future amount, and any interest rate:

$$PV = \frac{1}{(1 + R)^n} \times FV$$

Again, pocket calculators designed for business use have a function for the present value of a future amount built in. Table A–2 in the appendix also contains a few values of this function for convenience.

As a further illustration of the use of present value, assume there exists a bond that pays no interest, but can be redeemed for \$1,000 in six years. The interest rate on investments of this risk is presently 16 percent. Therefore, the most one would be willing to pay for the bond is:

$$PV = \frac{1}{(1 + 0.16)^6} \times \$1{,}000$$

$$0.410 \times \$1000 = \$410$$

The multiplication factor 0.410 was found by going down the 16 percent column in Table A–2 until the value for six years was found.

As can be seen from the analysis above, the present value of a future payment decreases as the time at which the payment is to be received becomes more distant and as the interest rate becomes higher. This relationship is illustrated by showing present values for two interest rates at various time horizons in Figure 7–1.

Value of a stream of payments

Many business decisions involve an expenditure today with the expectation of a series of receipts in the future. One can determine the value of the investment by finding the present value of each future payment and adding up these present values. Suppose a company has other investment opportunities that will earn 12 percent. A particular investment opportunity is expected to return cash of $1,000 in one year, $1,200 in two years, and $1,500 in three years. The question is whether the investment is worth its $2,500 cost. As was done with the single payment examples above, the present value of each cash flow is found and these present values are then added to find the present value of all the flows:

Year	*Cash flow*	×	*Present value factor from Table 2*	=	*Present value*
1	$1,000		0.893		$ 893.00
2	1,200		0.797		956.40
3	1,500		0.712		1,068.00
				Total	$2,917.40

The present value factor for each year can be found by solving for $1/(1 + 0.12)^n$ for each of the three years, by using Table A–1, or by using a calculator with a built-in present value function. In this particular case, the factors were found by going down the 12 percent column of Appendix Table A–2 to find the values for one, two, and three years. If the company were to pay $2,917.40 for the project, it would earn exactly a 12 percent return. Since the project can be acquired for

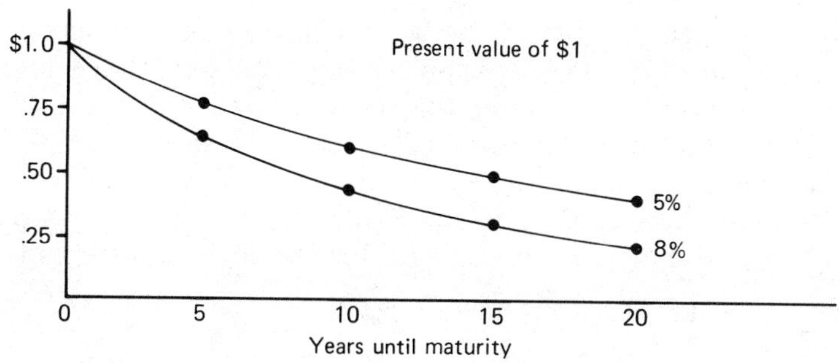

Figure 7–1 Interest rate, maturity and value

less, its return will be higher than on the 12 percent alternatives. Thus, the project would be attractive for a company that has 12 percent investment alternatives.

Although the above procedure gives the correct answer, it can be somewhat tedious. In analyzing situations in which the cash flow for each of a number of years is expected to be the same, a short cut is possible. Suppose, for example, the company had another investment opportunity that would provide cash flows of $1,000 per year for three years. At a 12 percent required return, the present value would be:

$$PV = 0.893 \times \$1{,}000 + 0.797 \times \$1{,}000 + 0.712 \times \$1{,}000 = \$2{,}402$$

Alternately, this can be written:

$$\begin{aligned} PV &= (0.893 + 0.797 + 0.712) \times \$1{,}000 \\ &= 2.402 \times \$1{,}000 = \$2{,}402 \end{aligned}$$

Hence, when the cash flow is the same each year, it is possible to add the present value factors from Table A–2 and then multiply this sum by the cash flow to find the present value.

The process of adding the present value factors first is useful, primarily because it creates the opportunity to create another table (or calculator function). Table A–3 in the appendix contains the sums of the present value factors from Table A–2. For example, the three-year factor in the 12 percent column of Table A–3 is the sum of the 12 percent value factors for the first three years in Table A–2. It can be used directly to find the present value of $1,000 per person for three years:

$$\begin{aligned} PV &= \text{present value factor from Table A–3} \times \text{annual cash flow} \\ &= 2.402 \times \$1{,}000 = \$2{,}402 \end{aligned}$$

The benefits of the latter approach are particularly significant when cash flows are expected to occur over a large number of years. Suppose, for example, the company had an opportunity that would generate cash flows of $3,000 per year for thirty years. Instead of doing thirty calculations, it is only necessary to look down the 12 percent column of Appendix Table A–3 and find the thirty-year value: 8.055. The present value of this stream of payments is:

$$PV = 8.055 \times \$3{,}000 = \$24{,}165$$

As with the other present value computations, this one can be readily handled using a pocket business calculator with a built-in function that will give the present value of a stream of equal annual payments. A stream of equal annual payments is frequently called an *annuity*. Consequently, the function on the business calculator is frequently called the "present value of an annuity" function.

These same concepts can be applied to determine the rate of return that is being earned when the initial cost and the series of receipts is known. If an investment opportunity costs $8,100 and will produce cash flows of $1,000 per year for ten years, the problem can be stated as:

$$\$8{,}100 = \text{present value factor} \times \$1{,}000$$

Dividing both sides of the equation by $1,000 yields:

$$\text{present value factor} = 8.100$$

Going across the ten-year row of Table A–3, a present value factor of 8.111 is found at 4 percent. Thus, the return on this investment is approximately 4 percent. Using a calculator with a present value function, the exact interest rate is 4.027 percent.

Present value of mixed cash flows

Many investment opportunities include cash flows that are combinations of annuities and single payments. These present no particular problem as present values can be added with no difficulty. As an example, take a corporate bond that will pay $1,000 at maturity, in twenty years. Meanwhile, the bond pays interest of $80 per year. The present value of the bond equals the present value of an annuity of $80 per year for twenty years plus the present value of a single payment of $1,000 twenty years from now. At a 14 percent required return, the present value of the bond is:

$$PV = 6.623 \times \$80 + 0.073 \times \$1{,}000 = \$602.84$$

The present value factor 6.623 is the twenty-year factor in the 14 percent column of Table A–3 and the factor 0.073 is the twenty-year factor in the 14 percent column of Appendix Table A–2.

Present value of an infinite stream

The value of an infinite stream of cash flows is a simple problem, yet it frequently bewilders people. Suppose $1,000 was deposited in an 8 percent savings account. The annual interest would be $80 (0.08 × $1,000): the savings account could provide $80 per year forever. If *PV* is the amount originally deposited; *R*, the interest rate; and *F*, the annual cash payment, the savings account relationship above can be generalized as:

$$F = R \times PV$$

If both sides of this equation are divided by *R*, the result is:

$$PV = \frac{F}{R}$$

To exemplify the use of this formula, a share of preferred stock pays a dividend of $8.00 per year and is expected to remain outstanding forever. The current required return on an investment of this type is 16 percent; therefore, the value of a share of the preferred stock would be $8.00/0.16 = $50. Stated another way, $50 invested in an account that pays 16 percent interest could generate $8.00 per year in interest payments forever.

Alternate compounding periods

Interest is frequently compounded on other than a yearly basis. A bank may advertise that interest on savings accounts is compounded quarterly, monthly, or even continuously. Quarterly compounding means that one-fourth of a year's interest is added to the account each quarter, and the interest for the next quarter is computed on that new balance. This raises the effective interest rate because interest is earned on interest sooner than would otherwise be the case with annual compounding.

The effective annual interest rate when interest is compounded k times per year is:[1]

$$\text{effective annual interest rate} = (1 + R/k)^k - 1$$

A bank advertises an 8 percent interest rate on savings accounts with interest compounded twice a year. Thus, the effective annual interest rate is:

$$\text{effective annual interest rate} = (1 + 0.08/4)^2 - 1 = 0.0816$$

In other words, 8 percent a year for one year with semiannual compounding is equivalent to 4 percent a year for two years with annual compounding.

Conclusion

Time value of money concepts are extremely useful for effective decision making in many areas of management responsibility, particularly situations in which some of the expenses or income associated with a decision occur over an extended period. The concepts have frequently caused people difficulty, partly because they require the use of complex sets of tables to solve problems. However, the concepts themselves are relatively simple, involving rearrangements of one simple equation:

$$FV = (1 + R)^n \times PV$$

In the remainder of this book, the primary focus is on the management decisions involving factors which affect the firm over a number of years. Time value concepts will prove extremely useful in resolving these problems.

---

[1] When continuous compounding is used, the effective annual interest rate is:

$$e^R - 1$$

R is the annual interest rate as previously defined and e equals 2.71828. For example, 8 percent a year compounded continuously is equivalent to 8.3287 percent compounded annually:

$$2.71828^{0.08} - 1 = 0.083287$$

Solved problems

Problem 1 You deposit \$5,000 in your savings account. The savings account pays 6 percent interest. If you do not make any withdrawals, how much will be in the account at the end of ten years? How long would it take for the amount in the account to double?

Solution The first part of the problem can be stated mathematically as:

$$\$5,000 \times (1 + 0.06)^{10}$$

By going to the 10-year row and 6 percent column of Table A–1, we find that:

$$(1 + 0.06)^{10} = 1.791$$

The answer, therefore, is \$5,000 × 1.791 = \$8,955.

Mathematically, the answer to the second part of the question is found by determining the number of years, n:

$$(1 + 0.06)^{n} = 2.0$$

Going down the 6 percent column in Table A–1 the value of 2.012 is found at twelve years. You will have slightly more than doubled your money by the end of twelve years.

Problem 2 How much would you be willing to pay for an investment that will return \$500 at the end of two years, \$750 at the end of three years, and can be sold for \$1,000 at the end of four years if you wish to earn 8 percent annual interest on your investment?

Solution This problem can best be solved by finding the present values of each of the three payments separately and then adding the present values together.

Year	*Payment*		*Factor from Table A–2*		*Present value*
2	\$ 500	×	0.857	=	\$ 428.50
3	\$ 750	×	0.794	=	\$ 595.50
4	\$1000	×	0.735	=	\$ 735.00
			Total present value	=	\$1,759.00

If you pay $1,759 for the investment, you will earn an 8 percent annual return.

Problem 3 A particular bond has a ten-year life, a $1,000 face value, and a 6 percent nominal interest rate paid annually. In other words, the bond will pay $60 at the end of each year for the next ten years. In addition, the bond can be redeemed for $1,000 at the end of the tenth year. If you wanted to earn 8 percent on your investment, how much would you be willing to pay for the bond?

Solution This problem could be reworded as follows:

a. What is the present value of $60 at the end of each year for the next ten years, discounted at 8 percent?
b. What is the present value of $1,000 received ten years from now, discounted at 8 percent?
c. What is the sum of a and b?

The solution is as follows:

a. From the ten-year row and 8 percent column of Table A–3, we find 6.710.

$$6.710 \times \$60 = \$402.60$$

b. From the 10-year row and 8 percent column of Table A–2, we find 0.463.

$$0.463 \times \$1{,}000 = \$463$$

c. $\$402.60 + \$463 = \underline{\underline{\$865.60}}$

If you pay $865 for the bond, you will earn an 8 percent annual return on your investment.

Problem 4 A machine will provide the following cash savings after tax. Calculate the present value of these savings, discounted at 10 percent.

Year	*Cash savings*
1	$2,000
2	3,000
3	2,000
4	4,000

Solution The solution to this problem is found by calculating the present value of each individual cash savings using Table A–2, and then summing these present values.

Year	*Cash savings*		*Factors from Table A–2*		*Present value*
1	$2000	×	0.909	=	$1,818
2	$3000	×	0.826	=	$2,478
3	$2000	×	0.751	=	$1,502
4	$4000	×	0.683	=	$2,732
			Total present value	=	$8,530

The present value of this stream of cash savings is $8,530.

Problem 5 Village National Bank pays interest of 4 percent compounded semiannually. If you deposit $1,000 in an account at Village National and leave the money on deposit for ten years, it will grow to what amount?

Solution Ten years at 4 percent compounded semiannually is equivalent to twenty years at 2 percent compounded annually. The factor from Table A–1 for twenty years at 2 percent is 1.486. The deposit will therefore grow to $1,000 × 1.486 = $1,486.

8
Capital budgeting

A capital investment is an expenditure that is expected to result in cash returns over a period longer than one year. Since some of these investments may have lives of 20, 30, or more years, they determine the characteristics and profitability of the company for many years. The scope of such investments is broad and ranges from research and development expenditures, training programs, advertising campaigns, and common stock of other companies, to purchases of drilling machines, trucks, ships, factories, and apartment houses.

As the list of capital investments indicates, capital budgeting is not the sole province of any particular management group; most managers are involved in decisions in which returns from present expenditures are expected to span a period of more than one year. Consequently, most managers can enhance effectiveness by improving their ability to analyze these situations.

Since the time commitment for capital investments is considerably different from that for current assets, it is necessary to use different methods of analysis. Generally, it is possible to liquidate current assets within a relatively limited time period; therefore, it is only necessary to consider the profitability from these investments over the near term. And although profitability is also the main decision criterion for capital investments, it must be measured differently when returns span a number of years. The time value concepts introduced in Chapter 7 provide the basis for measuring the profitability of capital investments.

The capital investment decision involves four main steps:

1. **Proposal.** The capital investment is proposed by a manager who feels that money can be profitably used for a project in his area of responsibility. A major part of the proposal development is the identification of all costs and benefits associated with the project, stated in terms of cash flows. Thus, the proposal includes a projection of the revenue-generating ability of the project as well as consideration of all expenses and tax implications. The success of the capital budgeting program depends on the quality of the investment opportunities identified and on proposals prepared by managers.

2. **Evaluation.** The expected costs and benefits are analyzed to determine if the project is sufficiently profitable in light of other investment opportunities available and of the amount the company must pay to raise money. If the project is large, it will also be evaluated regarding its impact on the company's risk and strategic position.

3. **Decision.** Based on the evaluation of the proposed project and comparison with other projects that have been proposed, company management chooses the projects for which money will be allocated.

4. **Post audit.** An effective capital budgeting system will also include a post audit of all projects to compare their actual profitability with that projected in the proposal. The post audit serves as a valuable learning tool. Knowing which projects achieved their expected profitability and learning why other projects did not can help management in refining evaluation methods.

Regardless of which part of the capital budgeting process a particular manager comes in contact with, familiarity with all phases will help to keep things in perspective and to improve effectiveness in the area he deals with. Each part of the capital investment decision process is discussed in this chapter.

The Project Proposal

Top managers of corporations normally identify proposal generation as the key to a good capital budgeting program. They refer to the quality of the proposal paperwork and, more importantly, to the quality of the projects themselves. Finding more profitable uses for the company's resources is a major challenge continually facing all managers; it cannot be achieved by the chief executive or the financial vice president, but depends on the creativeness of managers at all levels. To be effective in this area, a manager needs to know how to develop a proposal and how the profitability of a capital investment is evaluated.

Identifying the cost of a capital investment

The first step in developing a proposal is the identification of costs associated with the project. If the proposal is for the purchase of a piece of equipment, the initial cost may be simply the price quoted by a supplier. However, even in these cases, it is necessary to be certain that all costs have been identified and that all tax implications have been properly recognized.

One frequently overlooked cost is the start-up cost. If a company builds a new factory, there will nearly always be delays and additional expenses as problems are discovered and corrected. Likewise, a single piece of equipment must be delivered, installed and tested before it is put into use. In addition, there may be "bugs" to work out. Unless the supplier has agreed to absorb all of these costs, they should be included in the estimated cost of the project.

Another frequently overlooked cost is the working-capital commitment. If a project results in increased sales, it will also lead to increases in inventory and accounts receivable. Because these needs will continue as long as the higher sales level is maintained, they are part of the investment. If these parts of the investment are not recognized in the proposal, profitability will be lower than expected.

In estimating the initial outlay for a capital investment, it is important to consider any tax factors that might serve to increase or decrease the net cost. As taxes have become so complex, a proposal for a large capital investment should be evaluated by a tax expert. Nonetheless, the manager developing a proposal needs to be familiar with the general tax rules, at least.

With regard to capital investments, the *investment tax credit* is one of the major factors that must be considered. The investment tax credit may be up to 10 percent. As an example, assume that new production machinery will cost $100 million and will require a $50 million increase in current assets—a total investment of $150 million. However, working capital investments do not qualify as capital assets for the investment tax credit. Thus, the net cost is:

Cost of machinery	$100 million
less investment tax credit	10
plus working capital needed	50
Net cost of the investment	$140 million

The initial cost of the investment is also frequently affected by the sale or the scrapping of an old piece of equipment when a new one is acquired. If an existing asset is being replaced, the revenue from its sale can be deducted from the cost of the new asset. (Of course, income from the decision must also be the incremental income from replacing the old with the new.) The revenue from the sale of the existing asset should be net of taxes. If an item that has been depreciated is sold above or below its book value, the gain or loss is generally treated as an addition to or subtraction from regular income for tax purposes.[1]

As an example, a manufacturer intends to replace some manual drill presses with automatic units costing $30,000 each. The old units were purchased ten years ago at a cost of $10,000 each and have been depreciated to book values of $5,000 each. However, they can be sold for $7,000 each. The $2,000 gain over book value would be treated as ordinary income and taxed at the company's 46 percent marginal tax rate. Thus, the net proceeds from the sale of one of these presses would be:

Sale price of press	$7,000
less tax (0.46 × $2,000)	920
Net proceeds	$6,080

The $6,080 and the investment tax credit could then be deducted from the cost of the new machine to arrive at the net replacement cost: $30,000 – $3,000 – $6,080 = $20,920.

[1] Only the amount by which the sale price of the asset exceeds its original cost will be treated as a capital gain and be taxed at the lower capital gain rate. One other complication arises in that the company might be required to repay part of the original investment tax credit enjoyed when an asset is sold early.

Identifying the benefits from a capital investment

Income from capital investments comes from two main sources: increased revenue and decreased expenses. If a project is expected to increase revenues, the amount of the increase is primarily a question of sales forecasting.[2] Projecting costs associated with increased sales requires the collection of estimates from engineers, cost accountants, manufacturing managers, and marketing managers, and the compilation of this information in the form of annual income and expenses from the project. If a project is to reduce costs, the savings estimates are normally prepared by managers who are responsible for that particular area of operations; i.e., the data processing manager would be responsible for estimating the cost reduction associated with a more efficient computer.

A capital investment involves a cash payment now with the expectation of receiving cash back at some later date. Although income is important, it is not cash flow. Depreciation is deducted from income as an expense item even though it involves no payment to anyone. To find the cash flow a project will generate, income must be adjusted for these noncash items.

For example, consider a plant expansion that will result in the annual income changes shown below:

Sales increase	$300,000
Materials expense	100,000
Labor expense	100,000
Depreciation expense	50,000
Miscellaneous expense	20,000
Increased earnings before taxes	30,000
Increased income taxes	12,000
Increase in net income	$ 18,000

While most of the annual expenses associated with this project are in the form of cash, depreciation is not. Its impact is shown in the statement below, which includes one column for income and another for only the items affecting cash flow:

[2] One who is responsible for forecasting revenue would want to turn to a specialized book on forecasting techniques: William G. Sullivan and W. Wayne Claycombe, *Fundamentals of Forecasting* (Reston, Va.: Reston Publishing Co., 1977).

	Income items	*Cash flow items*
Increase in sales	$300,000	$300,000
Materials expense	100,000	100,000
Labor expense	100,000	100,000
Depreciation expense	50,000	
Miscellaneous expense	20,000	20,000
Earnings before taxes	30,000	
Income taxes	12,000	12,000
Net income	$ 18,000	
Net cash flow		$ 68,000

One might notice that the annual cash flow of $68,000 could also have been estimated by adding depreciation back to net income to adjust for the fact that it was earlier deducted, even though it was not a cash expense. Generally, it is possible to estimate cash flows by adding noncash expenses back to net income.

If the proposal involves replacement of one item with another, only the changes in cash flow should be used. If, for example, the preceding project involved the replacement of old equipment that would have been depreciated at a rate of $20,000 per year, the net increase in depreciation would then be only $30,000 and the analysis would appear as follows:

	Income items	*Cash flow items*
Increase in sales	$300,000	$300,000
Materials expense	100,000	100,000
Labor expense	100,000	100,000
Increased depreciation	30,000	
Miscellaneous expense	20,000	20,000
Earnings before taxes	50,000	
Income taxes	20,000	20,000
Net income	$ 30,000	
Net cash flow		$ 60,000

Identifying risk

The person preparing a capital investment proposal is faced with at least one critical factor about which an assumption must be made. For example, the exact level of future sales is seldom known.

Similarly, the profitability of a capital investment designed to reduce energy use will depend on the future cost of energy—something that can only be estimated. A method of recognizing the degree of uncertainty associated with a particular project is needed.

Informal analysis of risk is used by many companies. One method frequently used in informal analysis is to assign projects to broad risk categories. Projects involving gains in efficiency would normally be identified as low-risk; projects resulting in increased productive capacity in existing product lines would be identified as medium-risk; and projects involving new product lines or areas of business would be identified as high-risk.

Sensitivity analysis represents the most widely used approach to formally recognizing risk. If the manager is uncertain about the future cost of energy, he might identify the cash flows for the most likely energy cost, the lowest cost that has a reasonable probability of occurring, and the highest cost that has a reasonable probability of occurring. Likewise, an analysis that depends on a sales forecast might be repeated for several different levels of sales. Instead of a single estimate of cash costs and flows, several different estimates are prepared—possibly with an estimate of the probability of each outcome occurring.

Statistical analysis is a second formal method used by companies to measure the risk of proposed capital investments. Statistical measures such as the mean and standard deviation are sometimes used, as is computerized simulation analysis.[3] The purpose of any of these statistical methods is to state risk in terms that allow comparison among projects.

Evaluation of capital investment proposals

Once a project's cash inflows and outflows have been identified and a statement about risk has been prepared, the project's profitability is evaluated. Even if a manager does not have personal responsibility for evaluating capital investment proposals, he should know how they are evaluated. A manager who knows how proposals are evaluated will understand why certain decisions are made, will view his proposals more objectively, and will prepare more effective pro-

[3] For a discussion of the use of these methods, see Haim Levy and Marshall Sarnat, *Capital Investment and Financial Decisions* (Englewood Cliffs, N.J.: Prentice-Hall, 1978).

posals. The methods of evaluating capital investment proposals are outlined in the following chapters.

Present value analysis

In the preceding chapter, an investment was deemed attractive if the present value of its cash flows exceeded its cost. Present value analysis is no more than the application of this concept to capital budgeting. It is a widely used, effective method of evaluating capital investments.

As an example of present value analysis, assume that it costs a company 12 percent after taxes to raise funds. In other words, the required return for investment projects is 12 percent. (Determination of the required return is covered, in detail, in Chapter 9.) A project costs $100,000 after adjusting for tax considerations and will generate cash flows of $15,000 per year for ten years, giving a total of $150,000. However, it does not necessarily follow that the project is attractive; it is attractive only if the *present value* exceeds the cost. Using Appendix Table A–3, the present value factor for ten years in the 12 percent column is 5.650. Therefore, the present value of the project is:

present value = 5.650 × $15,000 = $84,750

Since the present value is less than the initial cost, the project is not attractive. Stated another way, the return on this project is less than 12 percent.

The computations are easier if the cash flows expected from the project are the same each year. However, the same general approach can be used even if cash flows vary from year to year. Assume, for example, that the company with a 12 percent required return is considering a project with a four-year life. This project costs $200,000, net of taxes, and cash flows in the four years are $70,000, $60,000, $90,000, and $50,000, respectively. It is only necessary to compute the present value of each of the cash flows independently and then add them to find the project's present value:

Year	*Cash flow*	×	*Present value factor**	=	*Present value*
1	$70,000	×	0.893	=	$62,510
2	60,000	×	0.797	=	47,820
3	90,000	×	0.712	=	64,080
4	50,000	×	0.636	=	31,800
			Total present value	=	$206,210

* From the 12 percent column of Appendix Table A–2

This project is attractive because its present value is greater than its cost.

The net present value is the present value of the cash inflows, minus the cost. In other words, it is the measure of the value the project adds to the firm. For the above problem, the present value was $206,210 and the cost was $200,000. Thus, the net present value was $6,210; investing in this project would be expected to increase the company's value by $6,210. The project considered prior to this one had a present value of $84,750 and a cost of $100,000, net of taxes. The net present value of that project would be minus $15,250 ($84,750 − $100,000). In other words, investing in the project would be expected to decrease the company's value by $15,250.

Although the costs in the previous examples were concurrent, many projects have costs occurring in later years as well. Fortunately, this presents no particular difficulty. The present value of a future cost is subtracted from the present values of benefits, in computing the net present value. For example, a project costs $100,000, net of taxes, and is expected to generate cash flows of $40,000 per year for its six-year life. However, it creates toxic wastes that will cost $100,000, after taxes, to dispose of during the seventh year. The company's required return is 14 percent. The net present value analysis is as follows:

Year(s)	*Cash flow* ×	*Present value factor* =	*Present value*
1-6	$ 40,000	3.889	$155,510
7	−100,000	0.400	−40,000
		present value	$115,510
		less cost	100,000
		net present value	$ 15,510

The profitability index is another measure based on present value. Stated simply, it is the ratio of present value to cost. If a project costs $100,000, net of taxes, and will generate cash inflows with a present value of $115,000, the profitability index is $115,000/$100,000 = 1.15. In other words, the project generates $1.15 of present value for each dollar invested.

Internal rate of return

Although the present value methods provide excellent measures of a project's profitability, some managers are not comfortable with the concept. They prefer to know what rate of return they are earning on a project. In addition to comparing returns between projects, they can compare the rate of return for a project to returns available in the investment marketplace, such as returns available on bonds. The widely used internal rate of return fills that need.

In the previous chapter, the return earned on an investment was determined by finding the present value factor that would make the present value of the benefits equal to the cost. This is all that is involved in determining the internal rate of return. Consider a project that costs $20,000, net of taxes, and provides cash flows of $3,000 per year for ten years. The first step in computing the internal rate of return is to find the present value factor (PVF) which will make the present value of the benefits equal to the cost. For this particular problem, it is necessary to find the present value factor that causes the present value of $3,000 per year for ten years to equal $20,000. The procedure is as follows:

$$\begin{aligned} \text{present value} &= PVF \times \text{annual cash flow} \\ \$20{,}000 &= PVF \times \$3{,}000 \\ PVF &= \$20{,}000/3{,}000 = 6.667 \end{aligned}$$

The second step is to determine the interest rate with which this present value factor is associated. Since it is associated with ten years, one only needs to search across the ten-year row of Appendix Table A–3 until the present value factor closest to 6.667 is found. As the number 6.710 is found in the 8 percent column, the internal rate of return is approximately (slightly over) 8 percent. Again, many pocket calculators designed for business have built-in functions to solve for the exact internal rate of return.[4] Using such a calculator, the internal rate of return for this project is 8.14 percent.

Unfortunately, the internal rate of return calculation is considerably more complex if a project's cash flows are not the same each year. Still, the approach is to find the interest rate which yields a present value equal to the cost. However, it must be found by trial and error, computing the present value of the project at various interest rates until the one that results in a present value equal to the cost is found. This process is illustrated in Table 8–1 for a project

---

[4] It is also possible to interpolate between two values in the tables. For example, the difference between the 8 percent and 10 percent value factors for ten years is 6.710 − 6.145 = 0.565. The difference between the 8 percent present value factor and the desired 6.667 factor is 6.710 − 6.667 = 0.043. The approximate internal rate of return is then:

$$0.08 + \frac{0.043}{0.565} \times (0.10 - 0.08) = 8.15\%$$

Table 8–1 Sample internal rate of return search

		8%		10%		12%	
Year	*Cash flow*	*PVF*	*Present value*	*PVF*	*Present value*	*PVF*	*Present value*
1	$2,000	0.926	$1,852	0.909	$1,818	0.893	$1,786
2	5,000	0.857	4,285	0.826	4,130	0.797	3,985
3	4,000	0.794	3,176	0.751	3,004	0.712	2,848
4	2,000	0.735	1,470	0.683	1,366	0.636	1,272
Present value			$10,783		$10,318		$9,891

that costs $10,000, net of taxes, and will provide uneven cash flows over a four-year period. As shown in the table, 8 percent was arbitrarily chosen as the starting point. As the present value exceeded the cost at 8 percent, a higher interest rate was needed. Ten percent was tried next, and the present value still exceeded the cost. Finally, 12 percent was tried, and the present value was less than the cost. Thus, the internal rate of return is between 10 percent and 12 percent. Since the difference between present value and cost is smaller for 12 percent than for 10 percent, one would correctly guess that the internal rate of return was closer to 12 percent.[5] Some pocket business calculators have the ability to solve the internal rate of return of a stream of uneven cash flows. Using one of these calculators, the internal rate of return is 11.477 percent.

The attractiveness of this project can now be compared directly to other projects of the firm. If the highest returns available in alternate investments were 10 percent, this project would be attractive. If there were sufficient projects available with returns higher than 11.477 percent, the project would not be attractive.

Payback period

Although most companies use one of the time value related methods discussed previously, some companies utilize other measures to obtain supplementary information. And even though the number is decreasing, a few companies still rely exclusively on one of these other measures—on the payback period, for instance.

[5] Interpolation can also be used in this case. The difference between the 10 percent and 12 percent present values is $10,318 – $9,891 = $427. The approximate internal rate of return is:

$$0.10 + \frac{318}{427} \times (0.12 - 0.10) = 11.44\%$$

The payback period is the number of years it takes the company to get back the money it invested. If a project costs $100,000, net of taxes, and provides cash flows of $30,000 per year for five years, it will have returned the original cost of the investment in three and one-third years: a payback period of three and one-third years. The project that costs $10,000, net of taxes, and provides the cash flows shown in Table 8–1 has a payback period of 2.75 years. This is determined by noting that the project will provide $7,000 by the end of the second year and $4,000 during the third year. Three-fourths of the third-year cash flows are needed to return the $10,000 cost, for a payback period of 2.75 years.

As a supplement to present value or internal rate of return analysis, the payback period provides useful information. In periods of tight money and high-interest rates, managers frequently want to know not only how long scarce money will be tied up, but also how profitable the project will be. Furthermore, the payback period is used in judging a project's risk. Since the future is always uncertain, the longer it will take to get the money back, the greater its exposure to uncertainty.

Accounting rate of return

The accounting rate of return differs from the measures discussed above in that it is based on accounting income rather than on cash flow. Stated simply, it is the average annual income from the project divided by its cost; hence, it is sometimes called the average rate of return. Consider a $50,000 project with a ten-year life that is expected to provide income of $5,000 per year during the first five years and $10,000 per year during the final five years. The average income is therefore $7,500 and the accounting rate of return is:

$$\text{accounting rate of return} = \frac{\text{average income}}{\text{cost}} = \frac{\$7{,}500}{\$50{,}000} = 15\%$$

The accounting rate of return is sometimes based on the average value of the investment over its life rather than on its original cost. If the asset in the above example was to be depreciated to its salvage value of $10,000 over its ten-year life, the average value of the investment would be:

$$\text{average value} = \frac{\text{beginning value} + \text{ending value}}{2}$$

$$= \frac{50{,}000 + 10{,}000}{2} = 30{,}000$$

The accounting rate of return by this method would be:

$7,500/$30,000 = 25%.

The accounting rate of return is not widely used as the primary decision criterion because it does not recognize the importance of cash flow. However, it is sometimes used as supplementary information because it provides a measure based on the income that the company must report to the shareholders.

Incorporating risk in evaluation

Keep in mind that risk is recognized in the proposal stage by subjective statement, by sensitivity analysis, or by statistical measures such as standard deviation. In the evaluation process, risk can be recognized by further refining the statement about risk or by adjusting the required rate of return for risk.

If the statements about risk are only to be refined further in the evaluation process, this leaves the ultimate recognition of risk to the decision process. The most common refinement is to compute the net present value or internal rate of return for each possible set of cash flows identified in sensitivity analysis. If statistical measures such as mean and variance are used, it is also possible to compute the mean and variance of the net present value or internal rate of return. These approaches simply supply the decision makers with additional information about risk.

Another approach is to use a higher required return for riskier projects. Many companies use one required return for projects that will increase plant efficiency, a higher required return for projects that will result in capacity expansion in existing product lines, and a yet higher required return for projects that involve new product lines. In addition, a company that has a number of different divisions might use different required rates of return for each division to recognize risk differentials between divisions. While there are some theoretical methods available for computing different discount rates, most companies using this approach rely on judgement in setting the required return for each type of project.

Capital budgeting decision

Once the proposal and evaluation have been completed, the decision must be made as to which project will be funded, and the first part of the decision process is the policy decision regarding who will have authority. Obviously, the chief executive officer of General Motors cannot analyze every request for a new typewriter; a substantial amount of authority must be delegated. In decentralized companies, the standard approach is to give authority for approval of various size projects at various levels within the organization. A plant manager might have the authority to approve projects costing up to $100,000 while a division manager might have authority to approve projects costing up to $500,000. Larger projects would then require approval of the company's executive committee or a capital budgeting committee.

In general, managers with authority to approve projects up to a certain size are given guidelines with regard to the criteria a project must meet before it can be accepted. For example, a company may authorize division managers to approve projects up to $500,000 in cost if the projects have internal rates of return of at least 14 percent. Since the manager will be evaluated according to return earned on investment, he has an incentive to invest in only those projects which he feels will be profitable. In periods of tight money or uncertainty, the company might supplement a minimum internal rate of return policy with a minimum acceptable payback requirement.

Whoever makes the decision must decide which project is more desirable. And, a project is desirable if the present value exceeds the cost or if the internal rate of return exceeds the required return. Thus, projects that are not desirable can be readily eliminated.

If the company has sufficient funds available, all projects that are desirable by the above standards can be accepted. A problem arises when all desirable projects cannot be accepted because the company has more good projects than money or because some projects are *mutually exclusive.* For example, a company needing more shipping capacity may face a choice between acquiring more trucks or installing a railroad siding.

One approach to choosing among desirable projects is to rank them by their internal rates of return. This approach is frequently adequate, yet presents potential problems. If a different required return is being used for projects of different risk, it is difficult to decide on a ranking between a risky project with an 18 percent internal rate of return and a low-risk project with a 12 percent internal rate of return. There are also ranking problems if the lives or sizes of two projects are substantially different. Would you prefer a project that earns 20 percent a year for ten years or one that earns 21 percent a year, but only has a one-year life? When problems of these types arise, a different measure of *relative* desirability must be used.

The net present value provides an excellent measure of relative desirability. Keep in mind that the net present value is the measure of the increase in value as a result of investing in a particular project. Consequently, maximizing the net present value will also maximize the company's value. Net present value is not so easily distorted by differences in product size or life; moreover, it is capable of handling problems in which different required returns are used for different levels of risk. All that is necessary is to choose projects in such a way that the net present value is maximized. For projects that are not mutually exclusive, a simple ranking by profitability index (present value/cost) achieves this purpose. If two projects are mutually exclusive, the one that creates the greater net present value is the one that is the more desirable. Because of these advantages, the net present value is particularly appealing when choices must be made among desirable projects.

Risk is incorporated in the decision process in either a formal or an informal way. The informal approach consists of simply applying some unspecified judgement when considering risk between two projects. If the statements about risk were informal, it is difficult to use anything else. The only alternative is to use subjective statements in assigning projects to broad risk classes, adjusting the required return according to risk class.

If more formal risk analysis, such as sensitivity analysis or statistical measures, was used, the decision process can be judgmental or formal. The judgmental method would once again involve weighing the information in some unspecified mental process. The formal approach would involve some specific way of assigning required return according to risk. In a few companies, modern portfolio theory and capital market theory are used to formally analyze risk.[6]

Strategic considerations. While the decisions about smaller projects may be based entirely on a desirability index such as the internal rate of return or net present value, larger projects involve the major strategic decisions of the company, thereby determining the competitive posture and products the company will have in the future. Consequently, top level managers use their own judgement as well as the information assembled in the proposal and evaluation phases when making these strategic decisions.

---

[6] For a detailed discussion of some of these methods, see Haim Levy and Marshall Sarnat, *Capital Investment and Financial Decisions* (Englewood Cliffs, N.J.: Prentice-Hall, 1978).

Post audit

In post audit, the outcome of a particular investment decision is compared to that envisaged in the proposal. Managers who expect this type of comparison to be made will be more concerned about the accuracy of the information in their proposals. Particularly, they will have much less incentive to underestimate costs and overestimate revenues in order to get pet projects approved. Furthermore, although few like to admit it, people are likely to be more diligent if they know that someone will be checking later.

A post audit carried out during the life of a project can also help in spotting developing difficulties and in taking corrective actions. The sooner a deviation from projections is spotted, the greater is the opportunity to take corrective action. These actions can range from changing policies or managers to selling the asset.

A post audit also serves as a valuable learning device. By learning why some projects were successful and others were not, managers can improve their ability to evaluate projects and assess risk. These benefits are not limited to companies experiencing difficulties. Just as there is no golfer so good that he can quit practicing, there is no company that has been so profitable that it can quit worrying about the quality of its capital budgeting decisions.

Conclusion

The primary consideration in evaluating capital investments is profitability. This is normally measured by identifying the cash costs and benefits, then evaluating them by computing the present value or internal rate of return. If a project is relatively small, the decision process may be a mechanical one of simply determining whether the expected profitability is higher than the minimum required. If the project is larger, the managers making the final decision will also take into account the risk, the quality of other projects, and the impact of the project on the company's competitive position. The character, financial health, and even the survival of a business can depend on the quality of the capital investment decisions made by its managers.

Solved problems

Problem 1 Midtek Corporation has a 10 percent required return. They are considering a new project that will require a $20,000 cash outlay and will provide after-tax cash flows of $4,000 a year for ten years. Compute the present value, net present value, profitability index, internal rate of return, and payback period.

Solution present value = $4,000 × 6.145 = $24,580.

net present value = $24,580 − $20,000 = $4,580.

profitability index = $24,580/$20,000 = 1.229.

The internal rate of return is found by a trial-and-error process of solving for the present value at various discount rates until we find the rate that gives a present value closest to the cost. For this project, the present values are computed at various interest rates:

Interest rate	*Present value computation*
10%	$4,000 × 6.145 = $24,580
12%	$4,000 × 5.650 = $22,600
14%	$4,000 × 5.216 = $20,864
16%	$4,000 × 4.833 = $19,332

Problem 2 American Manufacturing Corporation is considering a project that requires a $10,000 cash outlay and provides the following after-tax cash flows.

Year	*After-tax cash flow*
1	$2,000
2	4,000
3	4,000
4	6,000

Using a 10 percent required return, compute the present value, net present value, profitability index, payback period, and internal rate of return.

Solution

Year	*Cash flow*	*Present value factor*	*Present value*
1	$2,000	0.909	$1,818
2	4,000	0.826	3,304
3	4,000	0.751	3,004
4	6,000	0.683	4,098
		Total =	$12,224

present value = $12,224.

net present value = $12,224 − $10,000 = $2,224.

profitability index = $12,224/$10,000 = 1.2224.

payback period = 3 years.

The internal rate of return is found by a trial-and-error process of solving for the present value at various discount rates until we find the rate that gives a present value closest to the cost. For this project, the present values are computed at various interest rates:

Year	*Cash flow*	*Present value factor (16%)*	*Present value*
1	$2,000	0.862	$ 1,724
2	4,000	0.743	2,972
3	4,000	0.641	2,564
4	6,000	0.552	3,312
		Total =	$10,572

At a discount rate of 16 percent, the present value is still above the cost. Therefore, the internal rate of return is over 16 percent.

Problem 3 Midwest Manufacturing Corporation has the following investment opportunities. They have a total of $50,000 available to invest. Which projects should they choose?

Project	*Cost*	*Present value*
A	$10,000	$12,000
B	20,000	30,000
C	25,000	33,000
D	29,000	38,000
E	40,000	39,500

Solution You should choose projects in such a way as to maximize net present value subject to the limit of $50,000 available to invest. The net present values of the individual projects are as follows:

Project	*Cost*	*Present value*	*Net present value*
A	$10,000	$12,000	$ 2,000
B	20,000	30,000	10,000
C	25,000	33,000	8,000
D	29,000	38,000	9,000
E	40,000	39,500	− 500

Project E can be eliminated immediately since it has a negative net present value. Of the combinations possible within the $50,000 constraint, projects B and D are best. The selection of this combination will provide a total net present value of $10,000 + $9,000 = $19,000.

Problem 4 American Technical Corporation is subject to a 50 percent tax rate and a 10 percent required return. The company is considering a new finishing machine. The machine will cost $100,000 and will reduce materials waste by an estimated $25,000 a year. The machine will last ten years and will have a zero salvage value. Straight depreciation will be used. There is no investment tax credit in effect.

a. Identify the relevant cash flows.
b. Compute the present value, net present value, and profitability index.
c. Is this an attractive project?

Solution

a. The cash outlay to purchase the new machine will be $100,000. Annual depreciation will be $100,000/10 = $10,000. Annual cash flows can be identified as follows:

Annual material savings	$25,000	$25,000
Increased depreciation	10,000	
Increased profit before taxes	15,000	
Increased taxes	7,500	7,500
Increased profit after taxes	7,500	
Increased annual after-tax cash flows		$17,500

b.

Year	*Cash flow*	*Present value factor*	*Present value*
1–10	$17,500	6.145	$107,538

present value = \$107,538.
net present value = \$107,538 − \$100,000 = \$7,538.

profitability index = \$107,538/\$100,000 = 1.075.

c. This is an attractive project. It has a net present value greater than zero.

Problem 5 Southern Milling Corporation is considering a new automatic blender. The new blender would last for ten years and would be depreciated to zero over the ten-year period. The old blender would also last for ten more years and would be depreciated to zero over the same ten-year period. The old blender has a book value of \$10,000 but could be sold for \$15,000 (the original cost was \$20,000). The new blender would cost \$50,000. It would reduce the labor expense by \$6,000 a year. The company is subject to a 50 percent tax rate on regular income and a 30 percent tax rate on capital gains. The required return is 8 percent. There is no investment tax credit in effect.

a. Identify all the relevant cash flows for this replacement decision.

b. Compute the present value, net present value, and profitability index.

c. Is this an attractive project?

Solution a. Tax on the sale of the old machine:

Original cost	\$20,000
Sale price	15,000
Book value	10,000
\$5,000 × 0.50 =	\$2,500 tax on sale

After-tax cash receipts from sale of old machine:

Sale price	\$15,000
Taxes on sale	2,500
After-tax cash receipts	\$12,500

Net cash flow to replace old machine with new:

Cost of new machine	\$50,000
After-tax receipt from sale of old machine	12,500
Net cash flow to replace old machine with new	\$37,500

Depreciation on new machine = \$50,000/10 = \$5,000
Depreciation on old machine = \$10,000/10 = \$1,000

		Income items	*Cash flow items*
Annual labor savings		\$6,000	\$6,000
Depreciation on new machine	\$5,000		
Depreciation on old machine	1,000		
Increased depreciation		4,000	
Increased earnings before taxes		2,000	
Increased taxes		1,000	1,000
Increased earnings after taxes		\$1,000	
Increased after-tax cash flow			\$5,000

Year	*Cash flow*	*Present value factor*	*Present value*
1–10	\$5,000	6.710	\$33,550

Net present value = \$33,550 − \$37,500 = −\$3,950
Profitability index = \$33,550/\$37,500 = .895

c. This is *not* an attractive project.

Problem 6 Laclede Lighting is considering a new project. The company presently has sales of \$2,000,000 per year, total assets of \$1,000,000, net income of \$100,000 per year, net worth of \$800,000, and annual cash flow of \$110,000 per year. The company is not extremely sensitive to recessions. A modest recession would reduce annual cash flow by about 10 percent. A new project that will cost \$1,000,000 is expected to provide cash flows of \$170,000 per year for ten years. However, the project is extremely sensitive to recessions. A modest recession would result in a negative cash flow of \$100,000 per year. The firm's cost of capital is 10 percent. Is the project attractive?

Solution The net present value for the project is positive: \$44,650. However, the project is much more risky than the company's other investments. In a modest recession, it would reduce cash flow for the company to minus \$1,000 (cash flows for existing operations would decline 10 percent to \$99,000 and cash flows for the new project would be minus \$100,000). This would leave the company with substantial risk exposure. One approach would be to use a higher required return in recognition of risk. At a 12 percent required return, the project would have a net present value of minus \$39,500. A company would be unlikely to invest in such a project.

9
Required returns on capital investments

The required return is a key part of the capital budgeting process discussed in the previous chapter. Until the required rate of return has been determined, present value cannot be determined and the internal rate of return cannot be judged. In general, the appropriate required return to use is the cost of funds to the firm: the cost of capital. And the cost of capital is usually thought of as an *opportunity* cost; it is the return investors could expect from an alternative opportunity of equal risk. If a company is to compete successfully for money to invest, it must be able to earn returns that are at least equal to the returns on other opportunities available to investors.

Several important factors affect the firm's cost of capital. Because the cost of capital is an opportunity cost, one factor is the general level of investment opportunities available, which is reflected in the general level of interest rates. Another factor is that investors expect a higher rate of return if they are to be persuaded to invest in riskier assets. The more risk connected with the asset structure of the firm, the higher will be the return necessary to attract funds.

In addition to these factors, the company's mix of long-term sources of money affects the cost of capital. Because interest payments on debt are an expense for tax purposes, the payment of interest decreases the company's tax liability. Consequently, the inclusion of some amount of debt tends to lower the cost of capital. On the other hand, increases in the amount of debt lead to increased probability of default—failure to meet interest payments and repayment schedules. If the company has an excessive amount of debt, lenders must be compensated for this risk with a higher rate of return. This factor tends to increase the cost of capital as the amount of debt rises beyond some point. One of the goals in choosing the financing mix is to create the combination of sources of funds that yields the lowest possible cost of capital. The choice of a financing mix is taken up in Chapter 10.

In this chapter, the methods used to estimate the costs of various sources of funds are explained. These component costs are then combined to estimate the average cost of capital. This average cost is the average return the company must earn on its projects if it is to keep stockholders satisfied and compete for additional money in the marketplace.

To begin the discussion with a simple example, assume that a company has only one source of funds: bank debt. The company pays no taxes and pays interest of 16 percent per year on the bank debt. The company must earn a return of at least 16 percent in order to pay the bank. Thus, the cost of capital for the company is 16 percent.

But to develop a more realistic example, it is necessary to recognize taxes. Because taxes are so important to business decisions, they are recognized in capital budgeting by the use of after-tax cash flows. Likewise, the cost of capital is computed on an after-tax basis. Suppose the company in the previous paragraph had faced a 40 percent income tax rate. For every \$100 the company borrowed, it would pay \$16 in interest and, because interest is an expense for tax purposes, the company would reduce its tax liability by $0.40 \times \$16 = \$6.40$. Thus, the after-tax interest expense is $\$16 - \$6.40 = \$9.60$ per hundred dollars borrowed, or 9.6 percent. If K_d represents the after-tax cost of debt; R, the interest rate on debt; and T, the tax rate, this relationship can be conveniently stated as:

$$K_d = R \times (1 - T) = 0.16 \times (1 - 0.40) = 9.6\%$$

To make the example even more realistic, it is necessary to recognize that the company does not get all of its funds from one source. Suppose the company gets half of its funds by bank borrowing and gets the other half from its stockholders. Management has estimated (with methods to be discussed later) that stockholders could earn 20 percent elsewhere from investments of equal risk. Thus, the opportunity cost of funds raised from stockholders is 20 percent and because returns to stockholders must be paid from after-tax returns, this 20 percent is an after-tax cost.

Suppose this company raises a total of \$2,000, half from debt and half from equity. It must earn \$96 (0.096 × \$1,000) after taxes to meet the bank obligations and \$200 (0.20 × \$1,000) after taxes to meet the opportunity cost of money raised from stockholders. Thus, the average return the company must earn is:

$$\text{cost of capital} = \frac{\$96 + \$200}{\$2{,}000} = 14.8\%$$

This relationship can be stated more conveniently by letting K_e represent the after-tax cost of equity capital and by letting P_d and P_e represent the proportion of funds raised from debt and equity sources respectively:

$$\begin{aligned}\text{cost of capital} &= K_d \times P_d + K_e \times P_e \\ &= 0.096 \times 0.5 + 0.20 \times 0.5 = 14.8\%\end{aligned}$$

This 14.8 percent is referred to as the *weighted average cost of capital* because the costs of individual sources of funds are weighted by the proportion of total capital they represent. This is the after-tax return—the internal rate of return—the company must earn on its projects if it is to meet obligations to creditors and provide a satisfactory return to stockholders.

The computation of the weighted average cost of capital is reasonably straightforward once the costs of the individual sources have been determined. However, the determination of these component costs can sometimes be difficult. Methods of computing these costs are taken up in the next section.

Costs of individual sources of capital

The cost of each component of capital for a company is an opportunity cost, and it is the return investors could earn by taking the same risk elsewhere. Unfortunately, these opportunities are sometimes difficult to observe directly, particularly in the case of equity. Consequently it is frequently necessary to infer from their actions what investors view as the opportunity rate with regard to the company's securities. Thus, the focus of this section is on inferring the opportunity cost.

Cost of debt

The cost of debt is easier to observe directly than is the cost of other sources of funds. If a company borrows from banks or insurance companies at 16 percent, the cost of debt is 16 percent. It is only necessary to adjust this cost for taxes to compute the after-tax cost. Likewise, if a company is considering borrowing through the sale of bonds, investment bankers who handle the sale can tell the company what the interest cost will be.

An important issue in opportunity cost determination arises when a company has a bond issue outstanding that was issued when interest rates were lower than those presently prevailing. Suppose, for example, fifteen-year bonds were sold five years ago with an annual interest rate of 12 percent. These bonds were originally sold for $1,000 each and the holders will receive $1,000 (the par or face value) at maturity. Meanwhile, they will receive $120 per year in interest. However, interest rates have risen in the meantime such that new bonds of similar risk are paying in the area of 14 percent interest. Of course, no one will pay $1,000 for one of the 12 percent bonds when a 14 percent bond can be had for the same price. Consequently, the 12 percent bonds are presently selling for $896.00.[1]

If an investor buys the bond for $896 and holds it until maturity, he will earn a return greater than 10 percent on his investment. The return he will earn—the yield to maturity—is the internal rate of return of an investment with the cash flows provided by the bond. The yield to maturity can be determined by using a book of bond yield tables; by using a pocket business calculator with the necessary bond yield function; or it can be estimated by using a simple approximation formula:

$$\text{yield to maturity} = \frac{I + (P - M)/n}{(P + M)/2}$$

I is the annual interest paid, P is the par value of the bond, M is the market value, and n is the number of years until maturity. Applying this formula, the approximate yield to maturity is:

$$\text{yield to maturity} = \frac{120 + (1{,}000 - 896)/10}{(1{,}000 + 896)/2} = 13.8\%$$

[1] The value of a particular bond, given the required return, can be determined using present value analysis. See, for example, solved problem 3 in Chapter 7.

If the company were to raise new funds, it would have to pay a rate at least equal to the yield to maturity on the present bonds if it hoped to attract new money. Thus, the yield to maturity is the before-tax cost of debt. Suppose, however, the company has some money available that it can use for either new capital investment or repurchase of outstanding bonds. If the company were to buy back its bonds on the open market, it would not pay $1,000; it would buy them back for $896, thereby avoiding $120 interest per year and a $1,000 payment at maturity. The return to the company from this investment would be the same as that for any other investor purchasing the bond at the current market price. Thus, the yield to maturity is the before-tax opportunity cost of debt for this company whether or not it is considering the issue of new debt.[2] Of course, this number must still be adjusted for taxes. If the yield to maturity is 13.8 percent and the company faces a 46 percent tax rate, the after-tax cost of debt is:

$$K_d = 0.138 \times (1 - 0.46) = 7.45\%$$

Cost of preferred stock

Like debt, preferred stock carries with it a commitment to pay the holder a fixed amount each year. However, preferred stock differs in that (1) it has no maturity, (2) dividends to preferred shareholders must be paid from after-tax earnings, and (3) the preferred shareholders' claim is not as well protected as that of the debt holder. The features of preferred stock are discussed in more detail in Chapter 10. The focus here is on determining the cost of preferred stock.

Since preferred stock can be expected to remain outstanding indefinitely, the cost of preferred (K_p) is easy to compute from the market price of an existing issue:

$$K_p = \frac{D}{P}$$

Suppose a company issued preferred stock several years ago, promising an annual dividend of $10, and selling the preferred stock for its par value of $100 per share. Because returns on other investments have risen, the preferred stock is presently selling at $80 per share. As the opportunity cost concept also applies to preferred stock, the opportunity cost of the preferred stock is:

$$K_p = \frac{10}{80} = 12.5\%$$

[2] Administrative and sales costs associated with a new issue of a security will actually raise the cost a bit above the cost of existing funds from that source.

Since preferred dividends must be paid from after-tax income, this is the after-tax cost of the preferred. If a company does not have preferred stock outstanding at present and is considering selling some, the investment bankers who would handle the sale can provide a good estimate of the dividend needed to assure sale. A rough estimate can be made by looking at the cost of preferred stock for other companies.

Cost of equity

The cost of equity is the return required by the holders of the common stock. One might immediately suggest that because the common shareholders are the residual owners, having a claim to all funds that are not owed to others, there is no required return on equity. However, the same opportunity cost concepts that apply to debt and preferred stock apply to common stock. Shareholders purchased the stock of this company instead of investing their money elsewhere. And they made this decision because they believed they would earn a return at least as great as what they could earn in alternative investments of equal risk.

Failure to earn a satisfactory return for shareholders can lead to several problems. First of all, if returns on the shareholders' investment are less than expected, the price of the stock will fall because no one will want to buy it. Secondly, since many managers receive part of their compensation in the form of common stock or stock options, their wealth will be decreased. Another problem is that dissappointing earnings can make the company a likely candidate for an unfriendly takeover, in which the company's stock is acquired by another company and current managers are replaced. And even if a takeover does not occur, dissappointing earnings and falling stock prices make it extremely difficult to raise new equity capital that might be needed for expansion. Finally, there is always the possibility of different people campaigning for election as directors and gaining control of the company—normally firing existing management—if earnings are disappointing. Therefore, companies must be concerned about the required return on equity capital whether or not the sale of additional common stock is planned.

In the case of bonds and preferred stock, investors were promised a specific stream of payments and the market price of the stream was used to determine the required return. Since in the case of common stock there is no specific promised return to use, it is reasonable to assume that the market price reflects the equilibrium price, which causes expected return for this investment to be the same as that of equal risk opportunities. But there must be some method of estimating what the expected income is for that rate of return to be computed. Several approaches are used in making these estimates.

One widely used approach is the dividend growth model:[3]

$$K_e = \frac{D}{P} + g$$

K_e is the required return on equity capital, D is the dividend per share of common stock expected over the next year, P is the current market price of common stock, and g is the expected annual growth rate in dividends. Consider a company which has experienced very stable dividend growth of 3 percent a year. Dividends for next year are expected to be $10 and the most recent market price was $80. Using this formula, the required return would be:

$$K_e = \frac{10}{80} + 0.03 = 15.5\%$$

This approach is applicable for an established company experiencing a very stable growth in dividends since it is assumed that the growth rate will continue indefinitely. However, it cannot be used when dividend growth is not stable.

Another approach is to recognize that earnings per share represent the shareholders' income regardless of whether or not they are paid out in dividends or reinvested to provide greater dividends in the future. Using this approach, the required return on equity is:

$$K_e = \frac{EPS}{P}$$

EPS represents earnings per share and *P* represents market price per share.

If a company had earnings per share of $4 for the most recent year and its stock is presently selling for $30 per share, the estimated required return on equity is then 4/30 = 13.33%. If the price declined to $25, the estimated required return on equity would increase to 4/25 = 16%.

Though simple, this measure must be applied with care. The price of the stock reflects not only earnings for the past year, but also future earnings expected by investors. A very high ratio of past earnings to price might mean that future earnings are expected to decline

[3] For a proof of the correctness of this formula, see Fred Weston and Eugene Brigham, *Managerial Finance*, 7th ed. (Hinsdale, Ill.: Dryden Press, 1981), p. 595.

and that, therefore, the price has fallen. Of course, the converse—a very low ratio of earnings to price—may result from the bidding up of the price in anticipation of an increase in earnings. Because it is impossible to directly observe investor expectations, all measures of the required return on equity must be used with care.

Another measure of the required return on equity is based on recognition of the fact that the required return on any investment reflects the general level of interest rates and the risk associated with that particular investment. A widely used measure of the relative risk of an investment is the *beta*, a measure of sensitivity of return for a particular company's common stock to factors affecting returns on investments in general. Beta is illustrated for the common stock of a particular company in Figure 9–1. Returns (combined dividend and price appreciation) a holder of this particular stock would have earned, and returns the holder of a broad portfolio of stocks would have earned are observed during a number of time periods, such as months or quarters. Each dot in Figure 9–1 represents one set of observations. It can be observed over a period of time, that when returns on securities in general rise, returns on an investment in this particular company's stock also rise, and vice versa.

The line in Figure 9–1 is drawn to fit the sets of observations as well as possible; its slope is the stock's beta. Beta measures the expected change in return for this stock, per unit of change in expected return for stocks in general. From Figure 9–1, expected return for this stock is 3 percent if the expected return for stocks in general is 0 percent, and expected return for this stock is 7 percent if the expected

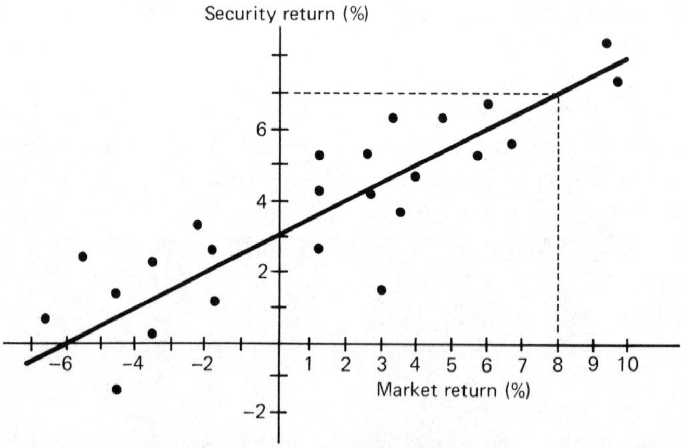

Figure 9–1 Illustration of beta

return for stocks in general is 8 percent. Thus the beta for the security is:

$$\text{beta} = \frac{\text{change in expected return for the security}}{\text{change in expected return for all stocks}} = \frac{0.07 - 0.03}{0.08 - 0.00} = 0.5$$

If this approach is to be used, it is normally not necessary to go to the trouble of computing a beta. Investment advisory services such as *Value Line* regularly publish betas for many companies, and are available at public libraries and brokerage firms.

The higher the beta, the more sensitive the returns on this particular security are to returns affecting market factors in general. A beta of 1.0 would indicate a stock of average risk. With a beta of 0.5, this stock has below average risk, and would therefore have a required return below the average for all stocks.

There is a widely recognized body of finance theory which suggests that the relationship between the beta and the required return is as follows:[4]

$$K_e = R_f + \text{beta} \times (E_m - R_f)$$

R_f is the return on risk-free investments such as U.S. government securities and E_m is the expected return from investments in common stocks in general. In general, the return on stocks has exceeded the interest rate on U.S. government securities by about five to six percent per year over extended periods of time.

To illustrate the use of beta, assume that a company has a beta of 0.5, that the yield to maturity on U.S. government bonds is approximately 12 percent, and that expected returns on stocks in general is believed to be approximately 6 percent above the return on U.S. government bonds. Using the beta approach, the required return on equity is:

$$K_e = 0.12 + 0.5 \times (0.18 - 0.12) = 15\%$$

Computing and using the weighted average cost of capital

The basic concept of the weighted average cost of capital was introduced at the beginning of this chapter. However, there are several issues that need to be considered when applying the concept.

[4] A proof and detailed discussion can be found in an advanced investment text such as Jack Clark Francis, *Investments: Analysis and Management* (New York: McGraw-Hill, 1980).

Book vs. market value weights

In order to compute a weighted average cost of capital, it is necessary to determine the cost of each component and the proportion of funds represented by each component. Because the market value of a security may be substantially different from its book value, it is necessary to decide whether it is the proportion of market or the proportion of book value that is the relevant measure. In general, the value of something is what someone is willing to pay for it. Therefore, it is reasonable to argue that a company's value is equal to the total of the market values of the claims against that company, including the market value of equity, rather than the sum of the book values of the assets. Applying this approach to the market value of the company, it seems reasonable to value its sources of funds at their market rather than at their book values in deciding what portion of the assets are actually financed by each source. The wisdom of this approach becomes evident when regarding a company whose equity is priced at several times its book value because the market value of the assets is worth substantially more than the book value. The market price of the equity—not its book value—represents the true portion of the assets financed by the shareholders since the assets could always be sold at their market values to return the money to the shareholders. Thus, the market value is normally used in choosing weights.

Consider a company with the following capital structure:

Long-term debt	$5,000,000
Preferred stock	2,000,000
Common stock ($1 par)	1,000,000
Paid-in capital	4,000,000
Retained earnings	5,000,000

Because the debt was issued several years ago when interest rates were lower, its market value is 80 percent of its book value, or $4 million. Rising interest rates have also caused the price of the preferred stock to fall, to 50 percent of its book value. The book value of the common stock includes the accounts labeled common stock, paid-in capital, and retained earnings—a total of $10 million. However, the market price per share is $5. Since the par value is $1 and the common stock account shows $1 million, there are one-million shares of common stock outstanding. At $5 per share, the common stock has a total market value of $5 million. The proportions of market value represented by each source are summarized below:

Source of funds	*Market value*	*Proportion of total*
Debt	$4,000,000	0.40
Preferred stock	1,000,000	0.10
Common stock	5,000,000	0.50
Total	$10,000,000	

The required return on debt has been determined to be 15 percent before taxes and 9 percent after taxes. The required return on preferred stock has been determined to be 16 percent and the required return on common equity has been determined to be 20 percent. Based on these proportions, the weighted average cost of capital (WACC) is:

$$\text{WACC} = 0.09 \times 0.40 + 0.16 \times 0.10 + 0.20 \times 0.50 = 15.2\%$$

A proposed project would be attractive if it had an internal rate of return greater than 15.2 percent or positive net present values when evaluated at a 15.2 percent required return.

Note that retained earnings were treated as part of common stock when the weighted average cost of capital was computed. The company has two types of owners' money, the first of which is money paid in by the owners, and the second is money earned by the company which was reinvested for the owners' benefit rather than being paid out to them immediately. The income earned on these retained earnings is part of the value purchased when one purchases a share of common stock. By computing the cost of equity, we have recognized the required return on the owners' investment regardless of form.

Average vs. incremental cost of capital

Occasionally, a project proponent will argue that the project should be evaluated at the after-tax cost of debt rather than the higher weighted average cost of capital because, at present, the company is raising new debt, not new equity. Nonetheless, it is important that a weighted average cost be used. The company can raise money through debt only because of the existence of equity; its capacity for borrowing depends in part on the amount of equity it has. And, every time money is borrowed, some of that capacity is used. The cost of that used up capacity should be recognized.

Using only the cost of the incremental funds being raised at the moment frequently leads to ludicrous decisions. Consider, for example, a company with an 8 percent after-tax cost of debt and a 20 percent cost of equity. Because the company is growing rapidly, its managers plan to fund its growth with a bond issue in January, a common stock issue in February, and another bond issue in March. Following the incremental approach, the company would happily invest in 9 percent projects during January, refuse 19 percent projects as being too low in February, and be happy with 9 percent projects again in March. This type of decision process will not maximize profitability. Even though incremental funding will cause the relative proportions of funds to change somewhat, weights equal to the average proportion of funds coming from each source should be used.

Cost of capital and required return

The weighted average cost of capital is the minimum acceptable rate of return for company projects with risk the same as the average risk for the company's existing projects. Thus, it can serve as the required rate of return for capital investment decision making, possibly with adjustments for risk. However, many companies base the required return on other numbers, such as historical returns on the company's assets or on a return objective desired by management.

One reason for using a required return rather than the weighted average cost of capital is that management does not have faith in the opportunity cost estimates developed. After all, the required return can only be estimated; it cannot be measured precisely. If managers are not confident in the cost of capital estimates, they may use their own discretion and set a higher rate of return "just to be safe." On the other hand, they may use a higher required return because they recognize that some projects will provide lower returns than expected and they want to be able to provide an average return for all projects equal to or greater than the weighted average cost of capital.

One danger with using arbitrarily higher required returns is that there tends to be a relationship between risk and return. By requiring such a high return, the firm may automatically filter from consideration the more stable projects and end up with a riskier set of assets. The increased risk then raises the actual cost of capital, and leads to another arbitrary adjustment of the required return and to movement into even riskier projects. Use of arbitrary required returns which are poorly conceived may lead to unplanned alterations in the company's risk.

Divisional cost of capital

When a company has several independent divisions operating in different markets, it is important that the cost of capital assigned to each division recognize the amount of risk in that division. The more risky division probably has the projects with the highest expected returns. Thus, if projects in all divisions are evaluated at the same cost of capital, funds are likely to flow almost exclusively to the most risky division. One way to avoid this problem is to estimate what the cost of capital for each division would be if it were an independent company. This can sometimes be done by computing the cost of capital for companies that produce the same products as that division. If this is done, an important accuracy check is to make sure that the weighted average of the divisions' costs of capital equals the corporation's weighted average cost of capital.

Conclusion

In order to evaluate the investment opportunities available, the firm needs a required return to use as a standard. The weighted average cost of capital represents the most widely recognized approach to developing a required return measure. The weighted average cost of capital is an estimate of the opportunities available to investors if they did not place their funds with the company. Although it is an estimate and must therefore be used with caution, the weighted average cost of capital is an extremely useful tool for assuring that profitability standards are met in the capital budgeting process.

Solved problems

Problem 1 ABC Corporation has the following capital structure. The company is subject to a 50 percent tax rate on regular income. Compute the before-tax and after-tax cost of debt, the after-tax cost of preferred stock, and the after-tax cost of common stock.

Debt

Market value: $2,000,000

Face interest rate: 7.1%

Market price per bond: $800

Principal value per bond: $1,000

Years till maturity: 20

Preferred stock

Market value: $1,000,000

Market price per share: $100

Annual dividend per share: $9

Common stock

Market value: $1,000,000

Market price per share: $80

Dividends for the coming year: $4

Expected continuous annual growth rate in dividends: 7%

Solution Cost of debt (before tax):

$$K_d = \frac{0.071 \times 1{,}000 + (1{,}000 - 800)/20}{(1{,}000 + 800)2} = \frac{71 + 10}{900} = \underline{\underline{9\%}}$$

Cost of debt (after tax):

$$K_d \text{ (after tax)} = 0.09(1 - 0.50) = 0.045 = \underline{\underline{4.5\%}}$$

Cost of preferred stock:

$$K_p = \frac{9}{100} = \underline{\underline{9\%}}$$

Cost of common stock (cost of equity):

$$K_e = \frac{4}{80} + 0.07 = \underline{\underline{12\%}}$$

Problem 2 Compute the after-tax weighted average cost of capital for ABC Corporation.

Solution

Item	*After-tax cost*	*Proportion*	*Weighted cost*
Debt	0.045	0.50	0.0225
Preferred stock	0.090	0.25	0.0225
Common stock	0.120	0.25	0.0300
	Weighted Average Cost =		0.075

Problem 3 If ABC issues new bonds, they will have a $1,000 face value, a 9 percent interest rate, and twenty-year maturity. Issue costs will be $100 per bond. For the preferred stock, issue costs will be $10 per $100 share. The company will receive $64 per new common share.

Compute the before-tax and after-tax costs of new debt, the after-tax cost of new preferred stock, and the after-tax cost of new common stock for ABC.

Solution Cost of new debt (before tax):

$$\frac{90 + (1{,}000 - 900)/20}{(1{,}000 + 900)/2} = 10\%$$

Cost of new debt (after tax):

$$0.10 \times (1 - 0.50) = 5.0\%$$

Cost of new preferred stock:

$$9 \div 90 = 10\%$$

Cost of new common equity:

$$(4/64) + 0.07 = 13.25\%$$

Problem 4 Compute the weighted average after-tax cost of new capital for ABC Corp.

Solution Cost of new capital:

Item	*After-tax cost*	*Proportion*	*Weighted cost*
Debt	0.05	0.50	0.0250
Preferred stock	0.10	0.25	0.0250
Common stock	0.1325	0.25	0.0331
			0.0831

10 Choice of financing sources

The two major financial decisions of a business are which investments to make and from where to get the money. The question of how to finance the firm's investments calls for less involvement from nonfinancial managers, particularly middle managers, than do the investment and spending decisions. However, knowledge of how financing decisions are made can improve the effectiveness of any manager. An understanding of the problems and issues faced in raising funds helps the manager to be more sensitive to both the constraints and the objectives affecting operating decisions.

When a company needs money to invest, the primary sources it can consider are borrowing, leasing of the assets it needs, selling preferred stock, and selling common stock. Within each of these broad types of financing, there are unlimited possibilities as regards the specifics of the arrangement between the company and those furnishing money. Considerations involved in choosing funding source can be broken down into three main categories: (1) the *cost* of the source of funds; (2) the *risk* arising from the requirement of a payment to investors even if earnings for a particular year are low or nonexistent; and (3) the *flexibility* to respond to changing conditions by buying or selling assets and by changing the financing mix.

In the first part of this chapter, the major sources of financing available to a business are described and evaluated with regard to their impacts on cost, risk and flexibility. In the second part of the chapter, methods for choosing the best financing mix are discussed.

Financing choices

As a group, corporations receive roughly half of their money by borrowing. Although specialized, leasing and preferred stock are important sources representing a relatively small percentage of total funds used by all corporations. Common stock and retained earnings are the other major sources of financing. The features of and the alternatives to each type of financing are discussed below.

Short-term debt

Trade credit is a source of funds to virtually all corporations, and a particularly important source of funds to smaller companies. Trade credit arises from the efforts of companies to encourage potential customers to buy, by not requiring them to pay on the day of sale. In many industries this practice has evolved to the point where standard terms of allowing some delay in payment are offered to all buyers who have acceptable credit ratings.

Credit terms and effective interest rates involved were discussed on pages 84 to 85. As illustrated by these earlier examples, trade credit can be a very inexpensive source of funds in many cases. Nonetheless, it can become very expensive when overused to the extent that a company damages its credit ratings or misses prompt payment discounts.

While many people argue that the firm granting credit must build the cost of credit into the cost of the product, the price normally does not depend on whether or not the buyer takes advantage of the credit terms. Therefore, it makes sense to take advantage of this source of funds. To do this requires awareness of several factors that can greatly affect the cost and availability of trade credit.

Willingness to negotiate credit terms is a frequently overlooked factor. The fact that a sales representative presents a standard printed price list and set of credit terms may not mean that the matter is closed. His briefcase may contain twelve different printed price sheets for the same product, not to mention his authorization to offer price discounts and extended credit terms if necessary to close the sale. The only way to take advantage of these opportunities is to be willing to negotiate and to be knowledgeable of industry practices.

Withholding of payment until the due date is another important way to take advantage of trade credit. While being one week late on thirty-day terms may cause problems, it is doubtful that a practice of paying one week early will improve upon a credit rating that can be had simply by paying on time. Smaller companies use a simple file system with all arriving bills filed according to the day they are to be paid; large companies achieve the same thing through computerized control systems. If money is available that is not otherwise employed and could be used to pay bills early, it might be better used for a temporary investment, such as a money market fund, until the expected due dates for bills.

Some companies extend their use of trade credit by not paying bills until they are well past due. Sometimes this is done as a temporary measure at the time of the year when the company has a peak need for funds, and at other times it is done because the company is in financial difficulty and has no other choice. Temporary stretching of accounts payable, particularly at the seasonal peak, can sometimes be done without serious damage to the credit rating. However, a policy of regularly stretching payables can have unfortunate consequences.

Since credit services such as Dunn and Bradstreet collect information about payment practices from current suppliers, a company runs the risk of damaging its credit rating if bills are not paid when due. In fact, the failure to take advantage of prompt payment discounts is usually a first sign that a company is getting into difficulty. Because the effective interest rate involved is frequently high, a company would not pass up prompt payment discounts if any other source of financing were available. A company with a damaged credit rating will find suppliers less willing to extend credit and less willing to grant price concessions.

Trade credit provides an attractive source of funds because it is convenient, readily available, and essentially free if used properly. However, excessive and improper use will make trade credit an expensive source of funds and will damage the company's credit rating to the point where other sources of credit become less readily available.

Accruals are expenses that have been incurred, but have not yet been paid; e.g., electricity used or the wages payable. Like trade credit, these sources should be effectively used by negotiating terms where possible and by not paying bills until they are due.

Notes payable are short-term loans from banks, finance companies, and other lenders. Because these notes carry maturities of under one year, they are normally used for temporary needs such as inventory build-up for peak borrowing needs.

A standard procedure with this type of borrowing is to establish a line of credit equal to the amount of anticipated borrowing need for the seasonal peak. The line of credit is a commitment by the lender to make up to that amount available. The borrower then draws against the line by borrowing when needed, frequently by calling the bank and asking that the amount currently needed be added to the company's checking account balance. Such notes are frequently "demand" notes which, in technical terms, require the borrower to repay the lender on demand. Of course, the lender is aware that the borrower needed the money for some use and could not have it available for repayment on demand. Frequently, the actual repayment plan is by informal agreement. Although many banks require or prefer that the loan balance be zero for one or two months out of the year, some demand that notes remain outstanding for years.

Banks establish a *prime rate,* which is the interest rate they charge their most credit worthy customers. When the prime rate is changed in response to a change in the general level of interest rates, the change is normally applied to all outstanding notes tied to the prime rate. Customers who the bank considers to be more risky are charged the prime rate plus one or more percentage points.

Notes may be unsecured or may be backed by the pledge of specific assets. Normally the most credit worthy customers are not required to pledge assets, as the loan is based on their ability to repay. When it is necessary to pledge assets for short-term loans, the two most common assets pledged are accounts receivable and inventory.

Pledging of accounts receivable gives the lender a claim against the accounts receivable if the company defaults on its loan. A loan secured in this way will be more expensive than an unsecured loan because the lender must evaluate the quality of the accounts receivable. *Factoring,* which is the selling of accounts receivable to a specialist called a factor, is an alternative to borrowing, and is expensive because the factor will normally pay an amount substantially less than the face value of the receivables. However, the factor normally relieves the company of credit evaluation problems.

Inventory can be pledged in a number of ways. A *blanket lein* gives the lender a claim to whatever inventory exists. It is normally used for work in process and for other situations in which the inventory is difficult to identify and segment. With *trust receipt* financing, also known as floor planning, the lender holds leins against specific serial-numbered items and is required to pay off a portion of the loan each time an item is sold. This approach is widely used by automobile dealers to finance their inventory of automobiles. *Field warehousing* involves setting off part of the borrower's premises as a designated warehouse area, technically under the control of the lender, to be used for storage of pledged inventory. Although the inventory is handled by company employees, its entry and removal is overseen by a representative of the lender. For example, a steel supply house might fence off part of the yard as a field warehouse for the storage of pledged inventory. *Terminal warehousing* provides the strongest security for the lender. Inventory is stored in a public warehouse and cannot be removed without the warehouse receipt, which is held by the lender as security. This approach is widely used for commodities such as wheat and frozen vegetables.

Commercial banks make both unsecured and secured short-term loans. Commercial finance companies, on the other hand, tend to specialize in secured loans. Some commercial finance companies specialize in accounts receivable security, offering either to loan against receivables or to act as factors. Others specialize in particular types of inventory lending. For example, finance companies owned by automobile manufacturers specialize in loans to retail customers and in floor plan lending to dealers.

Commercial paper is a very specialized source of short-term credit. It is available to only a relatively few companies, but is very important to some of those companies. Commercial paper is a short-term promissory note issued by a corporation with a well-known, very strong credit rating. Maturities range from a few days to 270 days. Companies either sell their commercial paper directly to buyers such as insurance companies or sell it in the open market through commercial paper dealers.

Commercial paper has the advantage of providing the borrower a slightly cheaper source of credit than does a prime rate bank loan. The main disadvantage is that although a bank will try to take care of its existing customers during periods of tight credit, there is no such feeling of obligation in the commercial paper market. For this reason, as well as to maintain their credit ratings, most companies that issue commercial paper maintain bank lines of credit equal to the amount of their commercial paper outstanding.

Intermediate-term loans

Depending on whose definition is being used, intermediate-term loans have maturities of one to five years or one to ten years. They are frequently made for the purpose of purchasing specific equipment, such as a truck, airplane, computer, etc. They are normally secured by the asset the money was used to purchase and they normally call for repayment by a series of payments over the life of the loan.

Intermediate-term loans are made by banks, commercial finance companies, and insurance companies. In addition, they are sometimes made by companies producing the equipment and by specialized lenders such as the Federal Intermediate-Term Credit Banks, which specialize in loans to farmers. Banks and insurance companies frequently cooperate in a single, large intermediate-term loan, with the bank taking the portion that will be paid off in the early years and the insurance company taking the portion that will be paid off in later years.

In recent years of high interest rates, many companies have issued bonds with intermediate-term maturities. However, these bonds have all of the other characteristics of bond debt, and are therefore treated as bonds.

Leasing

A company acquires an asset because it needs the service the asset provides, not because it needs to own the asset. Instead of purchasing the asset and making a series of loan payments, the company can lease the asset from its owner and pay a series of lease payments. Thus, leasing is viewed as a financing alternative.

Leasing became popular because the lease commitment did not show up on the balance sheet as a debt and because leasing allowed companies to circumvent loan agreements restricting further borrowing. While these original reasons have been largely nullified by changes in loan agreements and accounting rules, leasing has continued to be popular for other reasons. First of all, a lease frequently allows a company to finance the entire value of an asset while a lender may be willing to loan some lesser amount, such as 80 percent of the asset's value. Secondly and from the other side, someone who has leased an asset to the company will have less trouble reclaiming the asset in the case of default than someone who loaned the company money to acquire an asset.

Tax law is another major factor that has caused leasing to remain popular. Because the investment tax credit can be taken by either the lessor (owner) or lessee (user) of the asset, the lease provides an opportunity for a company that has a low tax rate to transfer tax benefits to a lessor in a higher tax bracket. The tax benefits can sometimes make a lease less expensive than a loan to the asset user.

Leases can be categorized according to service and financial leases. With a *service lease*, the lease price includes service and repairs. These arrangements became quite popular with computer installations, for example. In contrast, a *financial lease* provides credit and transfers tax benefits only. In a typical financial lease, the company selects the piece of equipment it wants and negotiates the price. Then a leasing company buys the equipment from the manufacturer and leases it to the using company, never actually taking physical possession. Normally the lease period covers the useful life of the equipment so that the leasing company avoids the problem of finding another user at the end of the lease period. While financial leases may be for specialized equipment, they are especially advantageous and popular for equipment that could be used by other companies in the case of default on lease payments. Airplanes and moveable offshore oil drilling rigs are frequently leased.

A service lease may be used as an alternative to ownership because of the service advantages: payment can be withheld if the equipment is not kept in working condition according to the contract. However, financial lease decisions are based primarily on cost. The company substitutes a series of lease payments for a series of loan payments, and must forego the tax savings provided by depreciation expense. In addition, it may forego the investment tax credit. The financial lease is chosen over ownership if the present value of the costs (net of tax benefits) associated with leasing is less than the present value of the costs (net of tax benefits) associated with owning.

Long-term debt: bonds

Long-term debt is used to finance a portion of the permanent funds needs of the firm. Companies arrange direct long-term loans from lenders, such as insurance companies, and they borrow from a large number of different sources by selling bonds. Direct long-term debt is similar to term loans with the exception of maturity. Therefore, the analysis in the following paragraphs is concentrated on bonds. A bond is a long-term promissory note. Individual corporate bonds are normally in denominations of $1,000 so that even relatively small investors can act as lenders. These bonds are sold to investors through the services of an investment banker, as explained in Chapter 11. A major advantage of the bond form is that although the company is guaranteed the source of money until the bond's maturity, the buyer of the bond can resell it in the marketplace if he should need funds.

Bond instruments. A bond itself is actually a single-page document indicating the amount owed to the holder, the interest rate, etc. The bond also makes reference to the indenture, a long document spelling out the details of the agreement. The indenture will identify the specific assets pledged as security and the details regarding early repayment. The indenture also contains a list of *restrictive covenants* which serve to protect the bondholders, as there may be restrictions on additional borrowing, sale of assets, and payment of dividends beyond a certain amount. Furthermore, the bond documents identify a trustee whose duty it is to act as the bondholders' representative in seeing that the company carries out its obligations as spelled out in the indenture.

Repayment. Bonds range in maturity from five to thirty or more years, with the shorter maturities having become more popular in recent periods of high interest rates. It is quite common to have some provision for gradual repayment between issue and maturity. One method of paying is through use of *serial bonds.* With a serial bond issue, part of the issue matures each year. A company might issue a series of bonds in 1982 with some due in 1988, some due in 1989, etc. Thus, payment is spread out and each individual bond holder knows when his bond will be repaid.

Another repayment plan is the *sinking fund* arrangement, calling for the company to pay the trustee a certain amount each year. Depending on the particular indenture provisions, the trustee invests this money until the maturity date of the bonds or uses it to buy back some of the bonds for the company before maturity.

Virtually all corporate bonds except those with the shortest maturities are *callable,* allowing the company to retire them prior to maturity if it desires. Although rising interest rates have kept companies from calling older, lower interest bonds in recent years, the flexibility given by the option to call is seen as important to corporations, which must deal with changing economic conditions. Usually, the company is required to pay some amount—a call premium—above the $1,000 face value of the bond in order to retire it early.

Some bonds are *convertible;* they can be exchanged for a specified number of shares of the company's common stock at the option of the bondholder. Since the value of the shares for which the bond can be exchanged is normally less than $1,000 at the time the bond is issued, the company views the convertible bond as a way to effectively sell additional stock above today's price. In addition, the company can pay a lower interest on its convertible bonds than would be required to sell a nonconvertible bond. A company that is considered a marginal credit risk may also find that the promise of convertibility is the extra sweetener needed to sell its bonds.

Security. The interest rate to be paid on a bond and the ability to sell bonds at all depends on how risky investors perceive the particular bond to be. Investors' perceptions of risk depend on the likelihood the company will repay and on the security available in the event the company does not repay on schedule. As with all debt, the main issue is ability and willingness to repay. Thus, many bond issues that are perceived by investors to be very safe do not offer the pledge of any specific asset. Bonds not backed by a lien on a particular asset are called *debentures.* In the event of bankruptcy, the debenture holders would share with other lenders a general claim against the assets.

Companies sometimes improve the credit evaluation of their bonds by pledging specific assets as security. The most common approach is the mortgage bond, backed by the pledge of specific property as well as the company's promise to repay. In the event of bankruptcy, the bondholders would receive the sale price of the pledged assets, up to the amount of their claim, and would have the status of unsecured creditors for any amount owed in excess of the sale price of the pledged assets.

Subordination is sometimes used when an earlier bond issue indenture placed restrictions on issuance of additional debt with an equal claim against assets in the event of bankruptcy. Holders of subordinated bonds would forfeit their claim to the creditors to whom they were subordinated, up to the point where the claims of those creditors were satisfied.

Bond ratings. Because many investors do not have time to do their own analysis of the company's credit worthiness, bonds are rated by several rating services. The interest rate a company must pay is affected by the ratings of its bonds. The rating system used by Moody's Investors Services appears in Table 10–1.

Eurobonds and foreign bonds. In recent years, companies have turned increasingly to the international markets to sell large bond issues. A *foreign* bond is one sold in a particular country and denominated in the currency of that country, but which is the obligation of a company headquartered in another country. An example would be a Japanese automobile manufacturer selling dollar-denominated bonds in the United States to build a factory in the United States. In contrast, a Eurobond is sold principally in countries other than the country in whose currency it is denominated. A number of American companies have recently used Eurobond financing, selling dollar-denominated bonds in numerous foreign

Table 10–1 Key to Moody's corporate ratings

Aaa

Bonds which are rated Aaa are judged to be of the best quality. They carry the smallest degree of investment risk and are generally referred to as "gilt edge." Interest payments are protected by a large or by an exceptionally stable margin and principal is secure. While the various protective elements are likely to change, such changes as can be visualized are most unlikely to impair the fundamentally strong position of such issues.

Aa

Bonds which are rated Aa are judged to be of high quality by all standards. Together with the Aaa group they comprise what are generally known as high-grade bonds. They are rated lower than the best bonds because margins of protection may not be as large as in Aaa securities or fluctuations of protective elements may be of greater amplitude or there may be other elements present which make the long-term risks appear somewhat larger than in Aaa securities.

A

Bonds which are rated A possess many favorable investment attributes and are to be considered as upper medium-grade obligations. Factors giving security to principal and interest are considered adequate but elements may be present which suggest a susceptibility to impairment sometime in the future.

Baa

Bonds which are rated Baa are considered as medium-grade obligations, i.e., they are neither highly protected nor poorly secured. Interest payments and principal security appear adequate for the present but certain protective elements may be lacking or may be characteristically unreliable over any great length of time. Such bonds lack outstanding investment characteristics and in fact have speculative characteristics as well.

Ba

Bonds which are rated Ba are judged to have speculative elements; their future cannot be considered as well assured. Often the protection of interest and principal payments may be very moderate and thereby not well safeguarded during both good and bad times over the future. Uncertainty of position characterizes bonds in this class.

(continued)

Table 10–1 (cont)

B

Bonds which are rated B generally lack characteristics of the desirable investment. Assurance of interest and principal payments or of maintenance of other terms of the contract over any long period of time may be small.

Caa

Bonds which are rated Caa are of poor standing. Such issues may be in default or there may be present elements of danger with respect to principal or interest.

Ca

Bonds which are rated Ca represent obligations which are speculative in a high degree. Such issues are often in default or have other marked shortcomings.

C

Bonds which are rated C are the lowest rated class of bonds and issues so rated can be regarded as having extremely poor prospects of ever attaining any real investment standing.

Source: *Moody's Bond Record*

countries. These bonds are used to take advantage of differences in interest rates and tax treatments among countries.

Preferred stock

Preferred stock has some of the characteristics of debt and some of the characteristics of equity. It is sold through investment bankers in individual share units as are both common stock and bonds. It carries a fixed dividend per year and normally (the exception being a seldom used form called participating preferred) does not participate in profits above this amount. An advantage from the company's perspective is that the commitment to pay preferred dividends is not legally binding. The stated dividend will be paid in a particular year only if the board of directors votes to pay it, and the preferred shareholders cannot go to court to force payment.

While the preferred shareholders cannot directly force the company to pay preferred dividends, they can bring significant pressure. Most preferred stock is *cumulative,* meaning that dividends cannot be paid to common shareholders unless the preferred shareholders have received their dividends for the current period plus any dividends that were due, but not paid, in earlier periods. In addition, there are frequently provisions giving the preferred shareholders the right to elect members to the board of directors in the event dividends have not been paid for a specified number of quarters. This would, of course, dilute the control of the common stockholders.

The par value of a share of preferred stock is the amount the holder would receive if the company liquidated, in bankruptcy or otherwise, and if there were money left over after all creditors were satisfied. Some preferred stock is callable, allowing the company to retire it by paying the holders the par value of their stock plus a specified call premium. Some preferred stock is also convertible; thus, it can be exchanged for a specified number of shares of common stock at the option of the holder.

Preferred stock has the advantage of being a fixed cost source of funds that does not subject the company to the risk of being forced into bankruptcy. The disadvantage is that, unlike interest payments, preferred dividends are not a deductible expense for tax purposes. The primary issuers of preferred stock are public utilities. The tax treatment is less of a problem to them because taxes are recognized as an expense in setting their rates. The primary buyers of preferred stock are property and casualty insurance companies. They like this investment because dividends received by a corporation are taxed at a much lower rate than is other income. This is important to the property and casualty insurance companies because they do not receive other preferential tax treatments.

Common stock

Common stock differs sharply from these other sources of funds in that the common stockholders are the owners of the company; the company is selling ownership when it sells common stock. As owners, the shareholders are not owed any income, but have a right to any income and value not specifically owed to others. In addition to their residual claim, the shareholders also exercise ultimate control over the company, primarily through the election of the board of directors. The shareholders also have the right to vote on certain other things such as changes in the bylaws of the charter under which the corporation operates.

All the company's earnings (after preferred dividends) are collectively owned by the common shareholders. However, the board of directors has no legal obligation to pay any of these funds out as dividends; the actual dividend paid to common shareholders each year is decided by a vote of the directors. Earnings not paid out in the form of dividends are reinvested in the company to increase both profits and dividends in the future. Consequently, together the dividends paid and the earnings per share are key numbers watched by investors. Other things being equal, an increase in expected earnings per share causes the price of the stock to be bid up in the marketplace. The owners' return is a combination of dividends paid to them and increases in the price of stock.

Control issues and the possible need to raise additional funds provide powerful incentives to management to work toward providing a satisfactory level of profitability to the shareholders. Another incentive is the fact that managers frequently own stock and receive options to buy additional shares of stock at a fixed price, so that their own self-interest provides incentive to pursue profitability.

Retained earnings

Since the proportion of earnings to retain for use in the business is a management decision (officially by the vote of the board of directors), retained earnings provide a source of investment funds. Managers are attracted to this source of funds because they do not have to go to outside markets for retained earnings. Of course, this does not excuse managers from market tests of their rates of return. Since shareholders can invest funds elsewhere if they are paid dividends, the company must be able to earn a return at least as high as that available elsewhere to justify reinvestment of the shareholders' funds.

Choosing sources of financing

In choosing the financing mix, the major issues to be considered are cost, risk, availability, control, and flexibility. Weighing these various factors with regard to each type of financing makes it possible to choose a financing mix that contributes to profitability while serving the other needs of the company.

Cost. To maximize profitability to shareholders, the firm needs to invest in the most profitable asset and finance those investments at the lowest possible cost. Debt has a cost advantage over equity in that the interest expense is deducted from taxable income; the typical large corporation's income tax is reduced forty-six cents for each dollar of interest expense. Of course, leasing has similar advantages. In contrast, dividends paid are not an expense for tax purposes and issuance of more common shares increases the number of shares among which earnings must be divided. Therefore, debt is normally attractive from a cost basis. However, continual increases in debt lead to the company's being viewed as more risky and, therefore, to the rising of the required interest. Minimizing the cost of funds involves the use of some debt, but not to the extent that the credit rating is jeopardized.

Risk. The perception that risk increases with increased debt is well founded. Because debt results in a fixed interest expense, it can further damage return to shareholders in periods of low profitability. Preferred stock has a similar impact: the preferred shareholders' dividend claims must be settled before there is any return for the common stockholders.

Beyond the question of expense items on the income statement, risk arises from commitments to generate cash flows. Interest must be paid as well as recognized, and scheduled debt repayments must be met. Given a specific amount of debt and a specific interest rate, the risk caused by the debt can vary greatly, depending on the cash flow commitment involved. A short-term loan requires cash for repayment in the near future, and this repayment is not an expense for tax purposes. For long-term debt, the cash flow commitment depends on the repayment schedule. Financial managers prefer terms calling for some or all of the loan to be paid at maturity rather than in annual payments in order to reduce the annual payment required. In general, financial managers pay as much attention to the cash commitment as to the actual amount of debt.

Availability. Since a company typically has on-going financing needs, it is important that a source of funds be regularly available. Reputation for loyalty during difficult periods is an important factor when choosing a bank lender. The difference between survival and failure for many contractors and real estate developers during recent tight money periods has been the willingness of their banks to work with them when properties were not sold on schedule. One reason commercial paper is backed up with bank lines of credit is that commercial paper has proved to be a very unreliable source of credit when questions about the company's credit are raised and when there are disturbances in the financial markets.

A company that follows the policy of borrowing the maximum amount possible may find available sources of funds very limited at later times. American Telephone and Telegraph has had a policy of not creating a debt level that would jeopardize its bond rating because its funds needs have been so large and so frequent that it needed access to new financing at all times. AT&T's management believed that this access could be ensured only by maintaining the highest possible credit rating.

Control. In many companies, top managers are concerned about their ability to maintain control of the company. They face risks of takeover bids from other companies and risks of controlling interest in the common stock being acquired by shareholders who wish to manage the company themselves or appoint different managers. They feel that selling additional common stock makes more shares available to those others who might wish to gain control. Use of debt is one way to avoid this problem. Risk of loss of control is also affected by the ways in which common stock is sold. Methods of distribution that decrease risk of control loss are discussed in Chapter 11.

Flexibility. Since it is not possible to foresee all future events, management must be able to respond to events as they occur. Therefore, freedom to act with the minimum number of constraints is a major consideration for all managers. A carefully thought out financing program can greatly enhance management's flexibility.

One aspect of flexibility is making sure that as many financing sources as possible will be available in the future. This is achieved by not being at an extreme point in the range of possible debt-to-total asset ratios. In the late 1960s, when stock prices were high by historical standards, many companies chose a strategy of borrowing the maximum amount possible and of avoiding stock sales while they waited for the price to climb even higher. They then found themselves in a period wherein stock prices had declined and borrowing was more difficult for all companies. In addition, they found themselves unable to turn to any market for funds and were forced to curtail growth, watching their market shares go to the companies that had maintained a more flexible financing strategy by not going to the limits.

Flexibility is also greatly enhanced by attention to the actual structure of financing agreements. For example, many companies accepted increased restrictive covenants in bond indentures as a cost of using higher debt ratios. Restrictions on future borrowing, changes in management, and sales of assets greatly reduced flexibility to respond to changing economic conditions. Virtually every bond issue includes a call provision, giving the company flexibility to repay the money before maturity if desired. Rapidly changing market conditions in recent years have made managers increasingly aware of the importance of arranging financing in ways that maintain flexibility.

Debt capacity

Implicit in the above discussion is the idea that there is some amount of debt the company can reasonably handle. Because of cost and control advantages, a company will normally wish to use as much debt as it can handle without becoming excessively risky and sacrificing flexibility.

Industry standard ratios provide one common method of determining debt capacity. Using this approach, the company should not exceed other companies in the industry with regard to certain debt ratios such as debt-to-total assets, times-interest earned, and fixed charge coverage. Some lenders are particularly fond of using industry average ratios as they represent the consensus of industry members as to the amount of debt a company can safely handle.

Bond ratings are also sometimes used as the standard for determining debt capacity. For companies that have large recurring capital needs and are continually selling additional bonds, this is a particularly useful guideline.

A problem with both of the above approaches is that they really defer to someone else's judgement in making the debt capacity decision; they provide no guideline as to what might actually determine a company's debt capacity. A direct method of measuring a company's debt capacity is based primarily on the company's ability to meet cash obligations associated with debt. Fixed charge coverage ratios give some indication, as do break-even points and cash flow break-even points. But a more direct approach is to use the techniques of pro forma analysis discussed in Chapter 5.

Miller Bakery Products provides an example of the use of pro forma analysis in measuring debt capacity. The president has read several newspaper articles suggesting the possibility of a one-year recession and is concerned about whether or not the bakery will be able to meet commitments associated with its present debt. The debt carries an 8 percent interest rate and calls for $3,000 a year in repayment. If a recession occurs, management feels that sales for the next year would decline by 20 percent. Although materials cost would decrease proportionally, the percentage decrease in labor would be only about half that of sales. Depreciation, overhead, and administrative expenses would remain unchanged. Replacement of worn-out equipment will require an investment of approximately $5,000 over the next year, with or without a recession. The ratios of current asset to sales and current liabilities to sales are not expected to change. The 1980 actual and 1981 pro forma income statements based on these projections appear in Table 10–2. The 1980 actual and 1981 pro forma balance sheets appear in Table 10–3 and show that

Table 10–2 Miller's Bakery Products

1980 and pro forma 1981 income statement assuming a modest recession

	1980 actual	1981 pro forma
Sales	$500,000	$400,000[1]
Cost of Goods Sold		
Materials	100,000	80,000[1]
Labor	280,000	252,000[2]
Depreciation	10,000	10,000
Overhead	20,000	20,000
Total	410,000	362,000
Gross profit	90,000	38,000
Administrative expense	40,000	40,000
Net operating income	50,000	(2,000)
Interest expense	2,400	2,160[3]
Earnings before taxes	47,600	(4,160)
Income taxes	23,800	(2,080)[4]
Net income	23,800	(2,080)
Dividends	0	0

1 Based on the anticipated 20 percent decline in sales and materials cost.
2 Based on the expectation that a 20 percent decline in sales would lead to a 10 percent decline in labor expense.
3 Interest declines because another $3,000 of debt is repaid.
4 Because of the tax loss carry forward and carry back provision of the tax code, the company would actually receive a reimbursement of $2,080 if the loss were as expected.

the company should have excess funds of $1,720 at the end of a one-year recession. Thus, the company has not as yet exceeded its debt capacity.

A critical part of debt capacity measurement by pro forma analysis is the choice of which adverse situation the company wants to be assured of surviving. If the adverse condition is defined as bad enough, no company can have any debt. For example, there is no debt level that will allow Miller Bakery to survive a ninety percent drop in sales each year for three years. Miller Bakery chose a one-year modest recession because this was the primary adverse condition that was presently of concern to economists. The decision as to the set of adverse conditions the company should be able to survive is a management responsibility.

The cash-flow approach to debt capacity again emphasizes the importance of debt cash-flow commitment as opposed to the dollar amount of debt itself. Structuring debt obligations to minimize the

Table 10-3 Miller's Bakery Products

1980 and pro forma 1981 balance sheets assuming a modest recession

	1980 actual	*1981 pro forma*
Cash	$ 2,000	$ 1,600[1]
Accounts receivable	5,000	4,000[1]
Inventory	14,000	11,200[1]
Total current assets	21,000	16,800[1]
Plant and equipment (net of depreciation)	75,000	70,000[2]
Total assets	$96,000	$86,800
Accounts payable	$12,000	$ 9,600[1]
Long-term debt (8% interest)	30,000	27,000[3]
Common stock	20,000	20,000
Retained earnings	34,000	31,920[4]
Total liabilities and net worth	$96,000	$88,520
Excess funds		$ 1,720

[1] Based on management's stated expectation that the ratio of current assets to sales and current liabilities to sales would not change.
[2] Beginning fixed assets of $75,000, minus depreciation of $10,000, plus new asset acquisition of $5,000.
[3] Beginning long-term debt of $30,000 minus scheduled repayment of $3,000.
[4] Beginning retained earnings of $34,000, minus the $2,080 loss for the year.

cash-flow commitment can substantially increase the company's overall debt capacity while decreasing its risk.

Conclusion

The company faces several major types of financing choices and, given the details of each financing method, an innumerable set of alternatives. A major management objective in choosing a financing method is profitability to the common stockholders, who own the company. However, this objective must be balanced with considerations of control, risk and flexibility. Debt should be structured so as to minimize risk and flexibility loss, per dollar of debt, as much as possible. Because debt is a lower cost source of funds, a commonly recommended approach is to determine the company's debt capacity by pro forma analysis and then set the actual amount of debt somewhat short of the extreme limit so that some flexibility is maintained.

Solved problem

In this chapter, the management of Miller's Bakery was concerned about the possibility of a one-year recession and prepared pro forma financial statements (Tables 10–2 and 10–3) which showed that the company had sufficient capacity to handle a one-year modest recession. Management is now concerned about the possibility of the recession deepening to a two-year recession with an *additional* 20 percent drop in sales in 1982. If this were to occur, no new equipment would be purchased in 1982. Furthermore, actions could then be taken to reduce the overhead and administrative expenses twenty percent from their 1981 levels. Depreciation would remain at $10,000, debt repayment would be $3,000, and interest for 1982 would be $1,920. Current assets, current liabilities and materials expense would maintain the same ratios to sales. Labor expense would decline an additional ten percent. Would Miller's have sufficient debt capacity to meet its debt obligations in 1982 if a recession unfolded in this manner?

Solution Miller's Bakery Products

1982 pro forma income statement assuming a deepening recession

Sales	$320,000
Cost of Goods Sold	
Materials	64,000
Labor	226,800
Depreciation	10,000
Overhead	16,000
Total	316,800
Gross profit	3,200
Administrative expense	32,000
Net operating income	(28,800)
Interest expense	1,920
Earnings before taxes	(30,720)
Income taxes	(15,360)
Net income	(15,360)
Dividends	0

1982 pro forma balance sheet assuming a deepening recession

Cash	$ 1,280
Accounts receivable	3,200
Inventory	8,960
Total current assets	13,440
Plant and equipment (net of depreciation)	60,000
Total assets	$73,440
Accounts payable	$ 7,680
Long-term debt (8% interest)	24,000
Common stock	20,000
Retained earnings	16,560
Total liabilities and net worth	$68,240
Excess funds	($ 5,200)

By the end of two years of recession, the company would have $5,200 less in funds than needed. Miller's does not have capacity to meet its financial obligations in a severe two-year recession. Since the company is scheduled to repay a total of $6,000 over the period, we can see that it would have the capacity to meet the interest payments, but the debt repayment schedule exceeds its capacity.

11 Market for investment money

Economists like to view a company in terms of its interactions with various markets: the market for its products, the market for raw materials, the market for labor, the market for managers, and the market for money. The choices available to the company are determined by supply and demand conditions in these various markets. Conditions in the market for money determine what investments the company can make and what rate of return it must earn. The description of the operations of the markets for the various types of funds will help in developing an understanding of the factors affecting individual business financial decisions.

Market for new stock and bonds

When a company wishes to raise money by publicly selling additional long-term securities, the marketing procedures are essentially the same whether the securities are stocks or bonds. In either case, the company sells the issue through the services of an investment banker. Investment banking firms are in daily contact with the financial markets so that they know what features—interest rate, price, restrictive covenants—will be necessary to sell an issue. In addition, they have the expertise to help with the complex paperwork involved and the contacts necessary to handle the actual sale of the issue. Finally, they are in a position to back their opinions about the saleability of an issue by guaranteeing that it will be sold.

Before getting into the process of sale, the question of who can publicly sell issues must be considered. Unfortunately, the fixed costs of selling an issue are quite high. The extensive legal work, including registration of the issue with the Securities and Exchange Commission, costs about the same for a million-dollar bond issue as for a billion-dollar bond issue. Therefore, the public sale of securities is only feasible for companies of substantial size. To sell $1 million worth of additional common stock might cost $150,000 or more in issue expenses. However, the cost declines from 15 percent of the money raised to about 4 percent as the amount raised increases from $1 million to the $100 million range. Issue costs as a percentage of net proceeds are substantially lower for bonds than for common stock, particularly for larger issues. However, they are still substantial enough to discourage small companies from entering into public sales. Some sources available to companies that cannot sell securities to the public are discussed later in this chapter.

Investment banking operations

When a company wants to raise money through either stock or bonds, the first step is choosing an investment banking firm. While investment bankers do not guarantee the quality of an issue to the buyers, their reputations are affected by the quality of the issues they sell. Therefore, they will thoroughly examine the company and decide if it has good profitability potential before agreeing to handle the sale. Certain investment bankers have more experience with some types of business than others and, therefore, may feel more capable of judging the company's soundness. In addition, some investment bankers handle only very large issues while others specialize in smaller issues. For these reasons, a company may find that one investment banker is reluctant to handle the sale of a particular security issue while others are happy to handle it. Although companies that raise money frequently tend to stay with the same investment banker, a company considering its first public issue may talk to a number of investment bankers before choosing one.

The initial discussion with the investment banker is called a *pre-underwriting conference*. At this stage, the type of issue (debt or equity) and characteristics, such as maturity and security, are chosen. The fee charged by the investment banker is also determined at this stage.

Once the company and the investment banker have reached an agreement, the issue is registered with the Securities and Exchange Commission (SEC). The issue cannot be sold until the registration statement becomes effective—twenty days after the registration statement is filed unless the SEC objects or asks for more time. The SEC studies the registration statement and determines if the appropriate information is being furnished to potential investors. The SEC does not rule on the quality of the investment, but on whether or not appropriate information about the investment is properly disclosed. The investment banker cannot sell any of the securities until the twenty-day period has passed, but can circulate a preliminary prospectus, commonly called a "red herring," explaining most of the features of the security. By widely circulating the preliminary prospectus, the investment bankers frequently have potential buyers lined up by the time the issue officially goes on sale.

Many issues are underwritten by the investment bankers. If the issue is underwritten, the investment bankers purchase the entire issue of securities from the company and then resell the individual securities to investors. In this way, the company has a guarantee that the entire issue will be sold. An alternative is the best-efforts arrangement, in which the investment bankers sell as much of the issue as possible, but have no responsibility for portions of the issue that are unsold. The best-efforts approach is used by companies that are so strong they are sure of the sale of their securities or so weak that investment bankers are unwilling to guarantee a sale. Because investment bankers guarantee the sale of most issues, they are commonly referred to as underwriters.

Risks involved in the purchase and resale of issues, frequently worth hundreds of millions of dollars or more, can be substantial. Therefore, the investment banker with which the company originally reached an agreement forms a syndicate of investment bankers and serves as the syndicate's leader. Each member of the syndicate agrees to purchase a certain portion of the issue for resale. Each member of the syndicate has its own selling group, which handles the actual contact with potential investors.

The buyers of new securities include both individual investors and financial institutions, such as insurance companies, mutual funds, and pension funds. Sale is achieved through announcement in the financial press and by direct contact. For example, an investor who is a customer of a particular stock brokerage firm and has previously invested in Aaa bonds may receive a call inviting him to invest in a new issue of Aaa bonds.

Although most features of the security are determined before the registration statement and preliminary prospectus are completed, the sale price is set just before the issue is actually offered for sale. Thus, the price can be adjusted in response to changes in market conditions. A rising interest rate in the marketplace may make a bond issue unsaleable at the interest rate stated in the prospectus. This problem can be overcome by selling the bonds a bit below their $1,000 maturity value in order to raise the effective interest rate.

Some choices available to the issuer

When a new issue of securities is to be sold, the company faces several choices. One of these choices is between underwriting and best efforts, with most companies preferring underwriting because of the risk that half an issue will be sold. A company that needs $200 million to build a new factory and only sells $100 million worth of securities is worse off than if it had sold nothing. It cannot build half a factory and the failure of its last issue will make it extremely difficult to sell another issue.

In the case of common stock and convertible securities, the company faces a choice between a *rights offering* and a direct public sale. With a rights offering, each shareholder is given an option to purchase a portion of the new issue equal to the proportion of the existing common stock he holds, at a price below the current market price. In many cases, the company must give existing shareholders an opportunity to purchase if the new issue is common stock or a bond that can be converted to common stock. In other cases, a rights offering is used simply because it is an attractive sale method. Since an option to buy stock below its current market price is valuable, a market for the rights will quickly develop, with stockholders who do not want to buy additional shares selling their rights. Almost all of the rights will be exercised unless the market price of the stock falls below the option price before expiration date. Since the rights normally expire in a few weeks, the price of the stock is not likely to fall enough to keep the company from getting the additional money it wants. With a rights offering, investment bankers frequently provide stand-by underwriting, promising to purchase any shares not sold through the rights offering.

In addition to making the sale easier, a rights offering has the advantage of causing the issue to be distributed to a large number of investors. This dispersion decreases control problems since no one person or group can get hold of the entire issue. When rights offerings are not used, the company selling common stock will want to discuss distribution plans with the investment banker to decrease the risk of some group using the new issue to gain control.

Secondly, the company has a choice between a private or a public placement of its securities. With a private placement, the entire issue is sold to one or a few investors, normally financial institutions. This method allows the securities to be tailored to the needs of the buyers and avoids the requirement that the issue be registered with the SEC. However, it provides no market for the securities in the event the original investor would want to sell them. Private placements are primarily used with bonds because companies prefer a broad distribution of common stock to keep any group from gaining a controlling interest.

Finally, the company must choose between selecting an investment banker through negotiation or through a bid process. The primary users of the bid process are public utilities, which are frequently required to solicit bids for services included in their costs for rate making purposes. When bidding is used, it is frequently necessary to contract with an investment banker for advice in the design of a marketable issue before bids are solicited.

Secondary markets for stocks and bonds: organized exchanges

The stock exchanges, such as the New York Stock Exchange, are the markets for securities that are of most interest to the general public. Their activity is covered in every local newspaper and every evening newscast. However, these markets do not provide a penny in investment money to corporations; they serve solely as markets in which existing holders of a company's securities can sell them to other investors. Nevertheless, a company is affected by the security prices determined by the bids of buyers and sellers in these exchanges.

As an aid to understanding, recognize that a stock exchange is only a meeting place for buyers and sellers, aided by communication equipment and "rules of the game." Neither the security exchange nor the company whose securities are being bought and sold have any direct roles in the transactions.

The operation of the exchange can be viewed by tracing a single order. An investor in Columbus, Ohio owns one hundred shares of General Motors common stock and, having read some depressing news about the outlook for the automobile industry, decides to sell this stock and look for a better investment. This investor calls the Columbus office of the brokerage firm with which he does business and informs the person who handles his account (commonly referred to as an account executive) that he wishes to sell. If the seller places a *limit order,* he sets a price and instructs the brokerage firm to sell the stock only if it can get that price. If the seller places a *market order,* he instructs the brokerage firm to sell at the best price currently available. In this particular case, the owner, eager to sell, places a market order.

The order is immediately sent by wire to the brokerage firm's office at the New York Stock Exchange. There, it is recorded and transferred to a representative of the brokerage firm who actually handles transactions on the floor of the exchange. That person goes to the location of the floor (referred to as a post) where General Motor's stock is traded.

Once at the appropriate post, the brokerage firm employee can sell the stock to the highest bidder among those representing people who want to buy. As an alternative, he can sell the stock to the General Motors *specialist* who maintains an inventory of General Motors stock and stands ready to buy or sell from that inventory, adjusting his prices according to supply and demand. The specialist makes a profit by buying for a few cents less than he sells for and by attempting to increase or decrease his inventory in anticipation of price changes. The existence of specialists assures potential buyers and sellers of a continuous market for their securities. Whether the brokerage house representative deals with the specialist or the representative of another brokerage house depends on which alternative offers the best price at the moment.

Once the agreement has been reached at the post, the only remaining detail is the back office job of transferring the ownership from seller to buyer, and the money from buyer to seller.

Prices in the exchanges are controlled entirely by the forces of supply and demand. If many people offer their shares of General Motors for sale while few people want to buy, the price will fall as sellers' representatives bid for the money of the few buyers and as the specialist adjusts his prices downward in light of current supply and demand. Equilibrium price will be reached as potential buyers find the stock attractive at the lower prices or as potential sellers decide to keep their stock rather than take the lower prices.

Note that the specialist has little choice but to adjust his price downward. If he did not adjust the price downward, he would need to stand ready to buy all of the stock of General Motors as well as that of the several other companies for whose stock he acts as specialist.

The price of an individual company's stock is bid up and down in response to changes in its expected profits and to changes in risk factors. If investors are to commit their funds, they must expect a return on this company's stock equal to returns on investments of equal risk. Likewise, the price of an individual company's bonds is bid up and down so as to change the effective interest rate in line with changes in the company's risk.

The prices of stocks and bonds as a group also rise and fall in accordance with overall supply and demand. An increase in expected inflation may cause some people who would otherwise buy bonds to use their own money plus borrowed money to buy real estate. The result is not only a decrease in the supply of money for lending, but also a decrease in demand for stock and bonds, which drives the prices of stocks and bonds down.

The prices of securities in these secondary markets are important to the company. If the price of bonds falls, the effective interest rates on those bonds rises. Should the company try to sell additional bonds, it would have to pay a rate at least equal to the effective interest rates on the existing bonds. Similarly, if investors feel the company's profitability outlook has declined, they will be less interested in owning its stock and the price will fall. At this lower price, the company will need to sell more shares of stock to raise the same amount of money. This further dilutes earnings per share and further decreases the stock's attractiveness as an investment. The whole process is reversed if increased profitability is expected. Consequently, the company is extremely interested in the prices of its securities in the secondary markets.

To help keep the prices of its securities up, a company can, first and foremost, make business decisions that maximize profitability and minimize risk. Second, the company can maintain a predictable dividend policy so that investors know what to expect. Third, the company can apply to have its securities listed for trading on an exchange so that investors will know there is a market, if they should later wish to sell their securities.

For a company's securities to be traded on an organized exchange, the company must apply to and be accepted by the exchange. When companies first become big enough that there is a market for their securities, the securities are normally traded on a regional stock exchange or on the Over-the-Counter Market (OTC). The OTC operates very much like the so-called organized exchanges except that communications are by electronic means rather than by meetings at a physical location. The two major organized exchanges have higher listing standards in terms of number of shares outstanding, value of the company's assets, etc. Of the two major organized exchanges, the American Stock Exchange (AMEX) has less-stringent listing requirements. Companies frequently apply for listing on the AMEX when they are big enough to meet those requirements, and then apply to the New York Stock Exchange when they have grown further. The New York Stock Exchange is the largest market, and there is a certain amount of prestige associated with being listed there, which may further enhance the market price of the company's stock.

Market for commercial paper

As explained in Chapter 10, commercial paper is a marketable, short-term promissory note with a maturity of 270 days or less, issued by a large company with an extremely good credit rating. About half of the commercial paper is sold to dealers, with the rest sold directly to lenders. Since most commercial paper is sold to financial institutions, a company might, for example, sell all of the commercial paper it wishes to offer to one or a few insurance companies, thereby avoiding fees.

Commercial paper dealers, of whom there are only a handful in the country, serve as buyers and sellers of both new and existing issues. In the case of a new issue, they purchase it and then resell portions to individual financial institutions. Although most commercial paper is held until maturity by the purchasing financial institution, an institution that wishes to resell can do so by selling to a dealer. A dealer differs from a broker in that the dealer buys and sells from inventory, like the specialist on a stock exchange, rather than directly bringing buyer and seller together.

Markets for direct credit

The markets discussed above are concerned primarily with the sale of securities to the public, with one company selling its securities to a number of investors. These markets are normally used for multimillion dollar security issues; companies needing smaller amounts cannot afford the costs of approaching these markets. Furthermore, large companies sometimes need to borrow quickly or need to borrow for longer than the maturity of commercial paper, but not as long as the maturity of bonds. In these cases, they will use the markets for direct credit.

Commercial banks are the most widely used source of direct credit. Although they specialize in short-term loans, they also make loans in the intermediate-term range. They loan money to both small and large businesses on both a secured and an unsecured basis. Because of their breadth of lending, commercial banks are often referred to as the department stores of business finance. However, they are not strong in long-term lending; they do not provide equity; and they normally limit themselves to loans of relatively low risk. Thus, some other lenders are also important.

Life insurance companies are particularly important in longer term lending. In addition to purchasing bonds, they make many direct business loans, with mortgage lending being an important part of their lending activity. Thus, life insurance companies serve a segment of the direct lending market not strongly served by commercial banks.

Finance companies specialize in secured lending, both short-and intermediate-term. Their short-term loans are secured by inventory and accounts receivable while their intermediate-term loans are normally secured by equipment that was purchased with the loan proceeds. They compete directly with commercial banks for some loans and make other loans that commercial banks would consider too risky. Of course, they compensate for extra risk by charging somewhat higher interest rates.

There are several distinct types of lending activity; some finance companies specialize in one type and others enter into a broader range of lending. Sales finance involves lending money to purchase equipment, frequently with the seller of the equipment also acting as the agent for the company handling the sales financing. In many cases, the seller effectively grants the credit and then sells the note (commonly referred to as dealer paper) to the company providing the financing. Banks compete with finance companies for the purchase of dealer paper. Factoring—the buying of shorter term accounts receivable—is done by specialized companies known as factors and by finance companies that handle factoring in addition to lending. As a group, finance companies provide a highly flexible set of financing sources for both fixed asset and working-capital needs.

Leasing companies also provide equipment financing by holding the title to assets and leasing them to the company. Leasing companies specialize in financial leases, in which the user selects the equipment and negotiates the price. The leasing company acts as financial intermediary only, providing the money for purchase. Many large banks have leasing companies as subsidiaries. Leasing companies vary from small companies that specialize in arranging automobile leases to large companies that specialize in organizing syndicates for leases to acquire assets costing hundreds of millions of dollars.

The Small Business Administration (SBA) provides a source of credit to small businesses. While the SBA makes a few direct loans, it normally participates with a commercial bank or guarantees a loan. The loans are for intermediate terms and, as the name implies, are limited to small businesses.

Small Business Investment Companies (SBICs) are a special type of company given preferential tax treatment to encourage the provision of private funds to small businesses. While SBICs can make direct loans, they prefer an arrangement such as convertible debentures which gives them an equity position. Because they hope to profit by selling these securities if the company is successful, their primary interest is in providing financing to companies with strong growth potential.

Venture capitalists include venture capital companies as well as individuals with funds to invest. They are interested in equity positions in promising young companies with good growth potential so that they can eventually make a capital gain on the sale of that company's securities. Venture capitalists are the usual source for filling the gap between the time a company can secure equity from managers, friends and relatives, and the time it is large enough to justify a public stock offering.

State and local industrial development commissions provide loans for the purpose of encouraging companies to locate and expand in their area, thereby increasing employment and the local tax base. They do this by issuing industrial revenue bonds, the interest on which is exempt from federal income tax for the buyers, and by lending the money to companies that agree to locate or expand in their area. The interest is frequently favorable because government units can borrow on a tax-free basis and because the purpose is to encourage the business to locate in the area.

Others. While the above list covers the major sources of direct funds, there are a number of other sources that occasionally provide direct credit. These include consumer finance companies, credit unions, employees, suppliers or manufacturers of equipment, pension funds, savings and loan companies, and various charitable foundations. However, none of these organizations is primarily in the business of direct lending to businesses. Pension funds are a rapidly growing source of funds to the economy, but most of their funds are used to purchase securities rather than to make direct loans. The Monetary Control Act of 1980 gave Savings and Loans the authority to expand beyond their traditional real estate lending base and to invest 20 percent of their assets in other types of loans and investments. However, they have not yet made any substantial moves because of the depressed state of the industry. Consumer finance companies and credit unions would only be indirect providers of credit by loaning to individuals who used their money for business purposes.

Approaching sources of money

When a bank loan officer is presenting a loan application to the loan committee, there is one key question: "How will the loan be repaid?" And equity investors want to know how they will get back not only their money, but also a profit. Successful raising of funds involves identifying the right sources of money and showing those sources just how they will be repaid. In order to provide this repayment, the company must achieve profitability and convert profits to cash.

Although the prospectus used in connection with a public offering such as a bond issue is supposed to answer the repayment questions, it is quite limited. Lawmakers wanted investors to be informed, but not misled. The repayment question requires projections such as pro forma financial statements. However, pro forma analysis requires judgement, opening up possibilities for misrepresentation. By requiring that the prospectus contain complete historical information, but no pro forma analysis, the problem of misrepresentation was handled. But to a large extent, this leaves investors to figure out how they will be repaid.

Companies approaching direct sources of money do not face the same restrictions. In fact, the pro forma analysis is likely to be the primary piece of information desired by many of these sources. Other essential information (such as product, market, and management analysis) serves primarily as a means by which the potential investor can decide on the likelihood of the projected profitability and cash flow being realized.

Conclusion

A financial manager approaching the market for money should be viewed a bit like a salesman for the company's product: he is not asking for pity or favors; he is dealing with people who want to make the best use of their limited resources. Like any salesman, he faces a broad market made up of many people with many different needs. He needs to know the market well enough to make contact with the particular investors whose needs will be met by their investing in this company. Then, he must convince the investors, who are themselves searching the market for investment outlets, that this company would indeed be the most advantageous outlet for their funds.

Of course, the normal situation is that the company does not face a single willing investor. If it is profitable, it normally faces a number of different money sources, each willing to provide funds on different terms. The scope of the financial manager's job extends from bringing around potential suppliers of money to deciding which set of financing terms is most beneficial to the company.

Cases for analysis

The case problems in this section provide an additional opportunity to apply the analysis techniques discussed in this book. As they are somewhat more complex than the solved problems at the end of the individual chapters, they serve as a bridge between the material discussed in the book and actual business problems.

Statewide Wholesale Grocery Company*
(Financial Statement Analysis)

Introduction. This case problem gives you the opportunity to look at a company from a lender's point of view.

Problem. The loan committee at Middle City State Bank was meeting to review the Statewide Wholesale Grocery Company account. Harold Yeager, a new loan management trainee, had been invited to sit in. The meeting was opened by Kirsten Brown, a senior loan officer, who said, "Jim Smith here tells me he's worried about the Statewide Wholesale loan. Now, my personal opinion is that Al Stephens down at Statewide would be contacting us if there was anything wrong. I know Al and worked with the loan officer who brought that account to us before he retired. Based on these men's characters, I would not question the loan then, nor would I now."

Smith expressed his concern about the year-end 1976 figures: "I ran a few coverages and they seem to be falling gradually behind over a period of several years. The current ratio is the main one that is low; it is below the two-to-one standard. Although we have no provision in the loan agreement to call the loan on the basis of ratios, we do have the right not to renew or at least to reduce our risk exposure when it comes up for payment or renewal next month."

Brown said, "Why don't we have Harold work up some figures on the wholesale grocery industry and meet us here a week from today?" They returned to their desks.

Statewide Wholesale Grocery, Inc. had been formed shortly after World War II by Al Stephens of South City and several independent grocers in nearby towns as a means of buying in volume to compete with the rapidly expanding grocery chains. Statewide quickly expanded its wholesale operations into the major distribution centers of the state. Stephens and his associates realized that there were strong, changing trends in grocery retailing that had to be planned

* Charles Franklin, Florida Atlantic University

for, such as a shift in emphasis from canned goods and other staples to frozen foods, baked goods, and to other perishable items. The firm had attempted to meet these challenges, even going heavily into wholesale nongrocery lines at one time. Rather than engage in the highly competitive retail business, they had decided to remain a general line wholesale grocer. They would sell on a statewide basis except in certain marginal products and in markets where competitive factors were against the firm. Stephens' business philosophy seemed to work reasonably well until the 1970s, when significant food price increases, partial regulation, shifts in consumer preferences, and continuing inflation added a high degree of uncertainty to normal operations. However, he was comforted that dollar sales had advanced so much under these circumstances, and that the company still made profits and paid dividends to its owners, who had all retired from their stores.

In the three days following the meeting, Yeager turned his attention to Statewide whenever he had an opportunity. He selected some ratios that he thought might be useful in analyzing a firm such as Statewide. He was still working on the calculations when Brown called him in for a progress report. He quickly reproduced a copy of his work up to that point (Exhibit 3) and took it to the meeting.

Analysis and questions

1. Finish the ratio analysis that Yeager started.
2. What are the financial strengths and weaknesses of Statewide Wholesale Grocery Company?
3. What action would you take as a bank loan officer?

Exhibit 1 Statewide Wholesale Grocery Co., Inc.

Consolidated income statement (in thousands of dollars)

	1974	1975	1976
Revenues, net	$43,494	$50,152	$62,334
Cost of goods sold	41,121	47,486	59,157
Selling and administrative expense	1,802	1,998	2,379
Interest expense	83	119	221
Depreciation and amortization	81	86	93
Total costs	43,087	49,689	61,850
Net income before taxes	407	463	484
Income taxes	185	211	220
Net income after taxes	$ 222	$ 252	$ 264

Exhibit 2 Statewide Wholesale Grocery Co., Inc.

Balance sheet, December 31

	1974	1975	1976
Current assets			
Cash	$ 280,000	$ 80,000	$ 85,000
Net receivables	1,510,900	1,624,800	2,076,600
Inventories	2,054,500	2,284,000	3,467,600
Prepayments	103,560	138,000	163,000
Property for sale	50,000	411,428	0
Total current assets	3,998,960	4,538,228	5,792,200
Fixed assets			
Properties, net of depreciation	655,680	673,500	704,280
Goodwill	210,840	210,840	210,840
Total fixed assets	866,520	884,340	915,120
Total assets	$4,865,480	$5,422,568	$6,707,320
Current liabilities			
Accounts payable	$2,058,360	$2,138,400	$2,778,720
Notes payable	344,780	632,520	1,136,860
Total current liabilities	2,403,140	2,770,920	3,915,580
Long-term bank debt	636,800	687,600	728,400
Total liabilities	3,039,940	3,458,520	4,643,980
Capital stock $5 par value	11,500	11,500	11,500
Paid in capital	48,400	48,400	48,400
Retained earnings	1,765,640	1,904,148	2,003,440
Total equity	1,825,540	1,964,048	2,063,340
Total liabilities and equity	$4,865,480	$5,422,568	$6,707,320

Exhibit 3 Statewide Wholesale Grocery, Inc.

Financial Analysis

	1971 Industry average	Statewide 1971	1972	1973	1974	1975	1976	1976 Industry average
Current ratio	1.8	2.0	2.1	1.9	1.7			1.9
Acid-test ratio	1.2	0.9	0.8	0.6	0.8			0.8
Ave. collection period	14.0	11.0	11.0	11.0	12.7			13.0
Cost of goods sold ÷ ending inventory	33.0	21.0	20.1	21.2	20.0			29.0
Sales ÷ net worth	13.2	25.0	24.0	26.0	23.8			13.2
Sales ÷ net working capital	14.8	24.0	24.0	25.0	27.3			16.0
Total debt ÷ total assets	0.62	0.61	0.63	0.64	0.62			0.69
Profit before taxes ÷ net worth	0.12	0.21	0.22	0.25	0.22			0.21
Profit before taxes ÷ total assets	0.050	0.076	0.079	0.078	0.084			0.074
Profit before taxes ÷ sales	0.013	0.009	0.009	0.009	0.009			0.014

Shaughnessy Cabinet Works
(Profitability Analysis)

Shaughnessy Cabinet Works, a manufacturer of wood kitchen cabinets, is considering adding maple butcher-block counter tops to the product line. The company has access to an adequate supply of maple and will market the counter tops to the retailers who handle their cabinets. Nielsen, the sales manager, pointed out that in some parts of the country 20 percent of new kitchen installations involved butcher blocks, and the percentage would be higher if adequate supplies of such counter tops were available. Shaughnessy felt that the recent surge in popularity, associatied with a general interest in "natural" products, would pass, and that in the long run not over 10 percent of the customers would select butcher blocks.

A bank loan of $200,000 would be needed to acquire the necessary machinery, inventory, etc. Fixed costs for the operation would be $20,000 per year, plus $16,000 interest on the bank loan. The counters would be sold to retailers for $6 per running foot, and the variable costs of production would be $4 per running foot. Shaughnessy's annual kitchen counter sales total 200,000 linear feet per year, creating a potential market for 200,000 linear feet of counter top.

a. Prepare a break-even chart for the proposed product line.

b. Would you recommend expansion into butcher-block counter tops?

c. The sales manager, Nielsen, suggested that preference, and not cost, is the reason for the choice of butcher-block counter tops. He felt that they could be sold for $7 a running foot with little impact on consumer demand. Shaughnessy was concerned that, at the higher price, retailers would simply carry another company's counter tops. Nielsen felt this would be a minor problem, certainly involving less than 20 percent of the retailers. Would the new product line look like a more attractive investment at the $7 per running foot price?

Midwest Furniture Imports
(Working Capital Management)

Roger Dukes began his career as a manufacturers' representative in the furniture business. Included in his lines were the products of several European manufacturers. This business gradually evolved into Midwest Furniture Imports, a wholesaling business that purchased fine furniture from European manufacturers and sold it to furniture retailers through a field sales force. By purchasing shipments of furniture in large quantity from European manufacturers, the company was able to negotiate more favorable prices and reduce shipping costs substantially. Furthermore, Midwest was able to assure delivery because orders could be filled from a Chicago warehouse rather than from a European location. When in 1978 Dukes retired and turned the business over to his son Melvin, sales had reached \$13 million a year and profits were in excess of \$400 thousand.

By late 1981, Melvin could see that sales for the year were going to be below \$13 million. Melvin decided to bring in an aggressive marketing manager who would get sales growing at a rapid rate again.

Melvin contacted an executive search company, which found Tom Bernstein. Bernstein had a record of frequent job changes, but had produced very rapid sales increases in each position. Bernstein stayed with Midwest only fifteen months (leaving in February 1983), but in that short time he was able to raise sales from \$12 million to \$18 million. Furthermore, profit increased by 40 percent in this one year. Even when Bernstein announced his resignation to take another position with a larger company, Melvin felt the decision to hire him had been an excellent one.

Melvin contacted the executive search firm again. This time they recommended Nancy Albright, a young woman who was presently a district sales manager for a furniture manufacturer. Albright was very interested in the job because it would give her greater responsibility for marketing policy. Since Melvin was so enthusiastic about the job that Bernstein had done, she asked what policy changes he had implemented to increase sales so dramatically. Melvin explained Bernstein's belief that merchandise availability was the key to furniture sales. Bernstein had insisted on increases in the amount of inventory carried by Midwest and had encouraged the retail stores to carry more by extending more generous credit terms to them. Specifically, he changed credit terms from 2/10, net 30 to 3/10, net 30 and established an unofficial policy of not pressing for collection as long as the merchandise was still in a store's inventory. The salesmen—who were paid a commission at the time of sale—were given the responsibility for reporting what inventory the stores actually held. In addition, Bernstein had implemented a change in credit standards so that the company could approve more new stores for credit. He felt that the old policy was biased against these new stores because they did not have a track record. Willingness to sell to this group had accounted for nearly half of the total sales increase.

Albright asked if this policy had weakened the accounts receivable. Melvin responded that he had been monitoring the days' receivables outstanding very closely and there had been only a very slight increase. Albright told Melvin that although she was very interested in the position, she could not make a decision until she had looked at the company's financial statements and had studied the status of its accounts receivable. Melvin was very hesitant to show this information to an outsider, but finally agreed to let her look at the records in the office. He allowed Albright to look at the income statements and balance sheets in Exhibits 1 and 2. In addition, she compiled the accounts receivable status summary in Exhibit 3.

Analysis and questions

1. Do you agree with Melvin Dukes that the quality of the accounts receivable has not deteriorated?
2. Rework the income statement on the assumption that 20 percent of accounts receivable over six months old are uncollectable.
3. Comment on the profitability and risk of the new credit policy.

Exhibit 1 Midwest Furniture Imports

Income statements
for years ending December 31, 1981 and 1982
(000 omitted)

	1981	*1982*
Sales	$12,370	$18,130
Cost of goods sold	8,659	13,054
Gross profit	3,711	5,076
Marketing expenses	1,237	1,894
Administrative and overhead expenses	1,833	2,127
Net operating income	641	1,055
Interest expenses	215	459
Earnings before taxes	426	596
Income taxes	170	238
Net income	$ 256	$ 358

Exhibit 2 Midwest Furniture Imports

Balance sheets
December 31, 1981 and 1982
(000 omitted)

Assets	*1981*	*1982*
Cash	$ 155	$ 148
Accounts receivable	1,562	2,543
less allowance for doubtful accounts	16	25
	1,546	2,518
Inventory	2,062	3,626
Current assets	3,763	6,292
Fixed assets	2,000	2,000
Total assets	$5,763	$8,292
Liabilities and net worth		
Accounts payable	$ 829	$1,215
Notes payable	310	2,325
Current liabilities	1,139	3,540
Long-term debt	1,500	1,500
Common stock	1,000	1,000
Retained earnings	2,124	2,252
Total liabilities and net worth	$5,763	$8,292

Exhibit 3 Midwest Furniture Imports

Accounts receivable summary
(000 omitted)

	1981		*1982*	
	Sales for period	*Sales for period that are still uncollected on December 31*	*Sales for period*	*Sales for period that are still uncollected on December 31*
Dec.	$1,484	$825	$1,994	$842
Nov.	1,360	305	2,176	504
Oct.	1,237	167	2,176	315
Sept.	1,113	78	1,810	173
Aug.	990	63	1,450	137
July	886	58	1,088	101
Jan. 1 to June 30	5,300	66	7,436	471

Finewood Arts, Inc. (A)*
(Pro Forma Analysis)

In 1970, Larry White, a building contractor in Kansas City, Missouri, hired Charles Klatt to build a book rack, a chart table and assorted woodworking items for his houseboat on Lake of the Ozarks in central Missouri. Klatt had recently graduated from Central Missouri State College in Warrensburg and was teaching manual arts in a suburban Kansas City high school. White was so impressed with Charles Klatt's craftmanship that he recommended him to several of his friends at the lake. By the end of 1972, Klatt was earning more money part-time than he was making as a teacher, and had expanded his product line to include handsome bar arrangements, gun racks, picture frames, and decorative shelving. To meet the growing demand for his services, Klatt had hired several of his former students at the high school to assist in the manufacture and installation of his products.

Early in 1973, White talked to Klatt about the possibility of going into business full-time with his financial backing. White felt it was important that Klatt have some equity in the business, and learned that Klatt had inherited some money from a deceased aunt and was in a position to invest between $50,000 and $60,000. With this encouraging news, the two began to plan for the establishment of Finewood Arts, Inc., with an initial capital of $200,000.

Both Klatt and White put up $50,000 in equity, and White purchased $100,000 in 15 percent mortgage bonds, with the plant and equipment pledged as collateral. The plant itself was built by White's construction firm and was located in Versailles, Missouri. Versailles was chosen as the plant site because of the availability of a former boat storage building and because of its access to the fast-growing Lake of the Ozarks region.

First-year sales exceeded $250,000 and by 1978 had reached $600,000. The major limitation on growth in sales had proven to be

---

* Jarold Abbott, Florida Atlantic University.

the ability to hire and train skilled craftsmen. Sales for 1979 were projected to increase by 10 percent without any increase in fixed assets or personnel. As chairman of the board, White was not actively involved in the operations of the business and was drawing a salary of only $5,000. Klatt earned $30,000 as president, and was the company's chief salesman, product designer, and plant manager.

It was apparent to White that the company had reached the limits of its growth without a major reorganization of the company. Such a reorganization would involve the expansion of the plant facilities, the development of a full-time sales organization, and the hiring of a plant manager. He felt that Klatt could best serve the company by continuing as president, while spending a greater percentage of his time in product development and in training craftsmen for the business.

Both White and Klatt had agreed that at least 50 percent of the assets of the company should be financed through equity, and that long-term debt should not exceed 35 percent of total assets. It was further agreed that approximately 50 percent of earnings after taxes would be reinvested in the business.

Prior to making a recommendation for reorganization of the business, White has reviewed the return on his investment to date. For his total investment of $150,000, his 1978 earnings included $15,000 in interest and $8,500 in dividends for a return of 15.7 percent. By adding in his share of the growth in retained earning, he calculated his return at 21 percent.

For a variety of reasons, including the fact that the company would be operating at capacity in 1979, White concluded that 1979 earnings would be representative of the long-term profit potential of the company. Before expanding his investment in Finewood Arts, Inc., he decided that it would be wise to compare the profitability of his construction business in Kansas City with that of Finewood Arts. He concluded that continued expansion of his construction business would be slightly less risky than that of Finewood Arts. Additional capital investment in his construction business would likely yield a return of approximately 25 percent.

With this in mind he decided to prepare pro forma financial statements for Finewood Arts for 1979. By doing this he hoped to anticipate total financing needs for 1979 and determine if retained earnings would be sufficient to provide needed equity. He planned to use the pro forma analysis to determine the size of the line of credit that should be established for 1979. In addition, he hoped to obtain an indication of the long-term profitability of the business. He hoped that the statements would indicate a return on his personal investment in excess of 25 percent (including interest, dividends, and his share of the growth in retained earnings).

In preparing pro forma statements for 1979, White reviewed the 1978 balance sheet and income statements with Klatt and with T. M. Bell, his accountant. Both Klatt and Bell agreed that the cost of goods sold as a percentage of sales should not increase in 1979. General selling and administrative expenses would probably increase in proportion to sales. As a first approximation, they assumed that the interest expense would not change from the 1978 level. Cash as a percentage of sales, average collection period, and inventory turnover for 1979 should be comparable to 1978. Plant and equipment are depreciated at the rate of 4 percent per year, with no additions to plant and equipment anticipated for 1979. Purchases of lumber and other raw materials are projected at the rate of $11,000 per month and are paid on terms of net 30. Short-term bank financing is expected to be available at an interest rate of 12 percent.

Exhibit 1 Finewood Arts, Inc.

Balance sheet for year ending December 31, 1978

Cash	$ 5,000	Accounts payable	$ 9,000
Accounts receivable	50,000	Bank loan	34,000
Inventory	58,000	Total current liabilities	43,000
Total current assets	113,000	Long-term debt	100,000
Fixed assets (net)	175,000	Common stock	100,000
Total assets	$288,000	Retained earnings	45,000
		Total liabilities and net worth	$288,000

Exhibit 2 Finewood Arts, Inc.

Income statement for the year ending Dec. 31, 1978

	(in thousands $)	
Sales		$600,000
Cost of goods sold:		
Materials	108,000	
Labor	220,000	
Depreciation	7,000	
Overhead	37,000	372,000
Gross profit		228,000
Less general and administrative expenses:		
Salaries	48,000	
Rent and utilities	24,000	
Advertising	60,000	
Miscellaneous expenses	12,000	144,000
Net operating income		84,000
Interest		18,000
Earnings before taxes		66,000
Tax at 50 percent		33,000
Net income		33,000
Dividends		17,000
Increase in retained earnings		$ 16,000

Finewood Arts Inc. (B)*
(Cash Budgeting)

Since its incorporation in 1973, 75 percent of Finewood Arts, Inc.'s working capital needs have been supplied by the First Marine Bank of Versailles, Missouri. Early in December 1978, Ben Luing, commercial loan officer for the bank, suggested that the company apply for a line of credit sufficient to handle its estimated working capital needs for 1979.

In response, Charles Klatt, president of Finewood Arts, asked that his accountant, T. M. Bell, prepare a cash budget for 1979. The cash budget would be used in support of the company's request for a line of credit, and would provide some indication of the company's ability to pay off or at least reduce the firm's current short-term indebtedness of $34,000. Bell based his preparation of the cash budget on Klatt's forecast of $660,000 in sales for 1979. Monthly estimates were as follows:

Dec. (actual)	$50,000
Jan.	30,000
Feb.	35,000
Mar.	45,000
Apr.	60,000
May	75,000
June	85,000
July	55,000
Aug.	55,000
Sept.	55,000
Oct.	55,000
Nov.	55,000
Dec.	55,000

One hundred percent of sales are for credit and are sold on terms of net 30. The experience of the company in collecting its accounts

* Jarold Abbot, Florida Atlantic University.

has been excellent, and Bell planned to base his estimate of receipts on the assumption that receivables would be collected within 30 days of sales.

Payments for raw materials, labor, utilities, overhead, advertising, miscellaneous expenses, and interest are generally made during the month following the time when the expenses are incurred. In anticipation of $660,000 in sales, the company planned to level out its production by producing an equal volume each month. Monthly expenditures for the year were estimated as follows:

	December 1978 actual	*Monthly 1979 estimated*
Cost of goods sold		
Purchases	$ 9,000	$11,000
Labor	18,000	20,000
Overhead	3,000	3,500
General selling and adm.		
Labor	4,000	4,000
Utilities	2,000	2,800
Advertising	5,000	5,000
Misc. expenses	1,000	1,000
Interest	1,500	1,500

Taxes are paid quarterly and will amount to $10,000 for the months of March, June, and September. Taxes to be paid in December are expected to total $11,500. A dividend payment of $4,000 has been approved for January. The April, July, and October quarterly dividend payments are expected to be $5,000 each. Fixed assets are being depreciated at the rate of 4 percent per year.

On January 3, 1979, Klatt called Ben Luing at the bank and requested an appointment for January 10 to discuss the company's line of credit. At the time of the phone call, the cash budget had not been completed, but based upon a projected balance sheet for 1979, Klatt told Luing that $20,000 should be sufficient to handle the needs for short-term financing. Luing was very pleased that the current short-term borrowing of $34,000 would be cut almost in half, and told Klatt that he was looking forward to reviewing the cash budget for 1979 on January 10. He further requested that Klatt mail him copies of the firm's balance sheet and income statement for 1978. These appear on page 184.

Buckey Products Company
(Required Return on Capital Investments)

In the past, Buckey products has used a 10 percent required return for all capital investment proposals. Although the 10 percent rate was decided upon by the executive committee a number of years ago, nobody can remember the reasons leading to the choice of a 10 percent figure. And although there is general agreement that the number should be re-evaluated in light of current conditions, there is no consensus about a new rate. In fact, there is considerable disagreement about how a rate should be chosen.

One member of the executive committee, Everett Roberts, has argued for the use of the after-tax interest on debt. "This is the rate we are paying for the last money we raised," he pointed out. The company's outstanding bond issue carries an interest rate of 12 percent and will mature in twenty years. The marginal income tax rate is 46 percent, so this would give an after-tax cost of 6.5 percent.

This number was immediately objected to on the grounds that the company could probably not sell 12 percent bonds again. "After all," pointed out Glen Brown, another member, "those bonds are presently selling at $880 rather than their $1,000 face value. We would certainly have to pay a higher return on new bonds."

"But we're not issuing new bonds," responded Roberts. "We're talking about a required return for investing money we already have."

"The money we have on hand didn't come from bonds anyway," joined in Laura Harper, the new marketing vice-president. "We are really talking about retained earnings. We should be using the required return on equity capital."

"If that's the case," said Roberts, "the required return is zero. We don't pay anything for those retained earnings."

A discussion ensued concerning the opportunity cost associated with retained earnings and other equity. Several methods were suggested for computing the return required by the shareholders. Some people were in favor of looking at earnings per share, some were in favor of looking at dividends, and one person had read something about a new method using a measure called beta.

David Vincel, the vice-president in charge of production, objected to the entire approach: "The important thing is to show investors that we are steadily improving. Our earning power is presently 18 percent. We should be looking for projects that will improve that number. If you want to talk about after-tax returns, we need 9 or 10 percent as a minimum acceptable return."

Finally, Neil Brokman, the president, said "It doesn't look to me like we are going to reach a consensus this way. Hendricks, this problem ought to fall primarily in your area as chief financial officer. Would you work up a memo outlining the possibilities and recommending an approach? That should lead to a more meaningful discussion."

The next day, Jim Hendricks, the financial vice-president, asked his assistant, Bill Proffit to begin collecting some information on the cost of capital issue. Proffit noted that the stock was presently selling for $20 per share. Dividends were expected to be $2.00 for the next year and had been growing at 6 percent a year. Earnings per share for the most recent year were $3.50. Proffit also noted that U.S. Government bonds were presently selling to yield 13 percent and the company had a beta, as reported by an investment advisory service, of 0.9. An article he had recently read indicated that the average expected return for common stocks, in general, was estimated to be about 18 percent, or about 5 percent above the risk-free rate. Proffit also noticed that the preferred stock, which paid an annual dividend of $10, was presently selling for $70 a share.

Analysis and questions

1. Which approach to the required return—historical return, interest on old debt, interest on new debt, or cost of equity—should be used? Why?
2. Estimate the required return on equity from the information given.
3. In determining a weighted average cost of capital, should the weights be based on the market or book values of the company's securities?
4. What required return do you recommend for Buckey Products?

Exhibit 1 Buckey Products

Balance sheet
December 31, 1982

Current assets	$15,908,000	Current liabilities	$ 6,280,000
Fixed assets	31,642,000	Long-term debt (bonds)	20,000,000
		Stockholders' investment	
		Preferred stock ($100 par)	5,000,000
		Common stock ($1 par)	1,000,000
		Capital in excess of par	9,000,000
		Accumulated retained earnings	6,270,000
Total assets	$47,550,000	Total liabilities and net worth	$47,550,000

IHT Corporation
(Debt Capacity Analysis)

The managers of IHT Corporation are interested in the risk of the company's capital structure. Specifically, they want to know if the company could meet its debt obligations in the face of a 20 percent sales decline. The company has a debt payment of $200,000 due each year. Long-term debt will be $2 million at the end of 1983 and interest expense for 1983 will be $168,000.

The production manager has estimated that the cost of goods sold would remain the same percentage of sales, and that the fixed operating expenses would remain constant at $3 million, even if sales declined. He also estimates that fixed assets, net of depreciation, could be reduced to $3,900,000 by not replacing certain equipment as it wore out.

The credit manager has estimated that accounts receivable turnover would decrease to 5-1/3 under these conditions. The marketing vice-president has indicated that it would not be possible to decrease the inventory level in the face of declining sales. The best that could be done would be to hold the inventory constant and avoid stockpiling.

Because purchases would decrease, it would be necessary to decrease current liabilities by 10 percent. The cash balance could safely be reduced by 10 percent. For simplicity, assume that all income will be taxed at 50 percent.

As a further analysis, management is interested in what would happen if sales remained at this lower level for another year. It is estimated that Net Operating Income would be the same in the second year of lower sales as in the first. With another $200,000 debt repayment, interest expense would decline to $152,000 in the second year. Cash and accounts receivable could not be reduced further, but inventory could be decreased by 10 percent. Fixed assets, net of depreciation, could not be reduced below the $3,900,000 level.

Questions

1. Will the company be able to meet its financial obligations in the face of a 20 percent decline in sales?
2. If sales stayed at this lower level for a second year, would the company be able to meet its 1984 debt repayment obligations?

Exhibit 1 IHT Corporation

Income statement year ending December 31, 1982 (000 omitted)

Sales	$10,000
Cost of goods sold	6,000
Gross profit	4,000
Fixed operating costs	3,000
Net operating income	1,000
Interest	184
Earnings before taxes	816
Taxes	408
Net income	$ 408
Dividends	$ 204
Increase in retained earnings	$ 204

Exhibit 2 IHT Corporation

Balance sheet December 31, 1982 (000 omitted)

Cash	$ 200
Accounts receivable	1,800
Inventory	2,000
Total current assets	4,000
Fixed assets (net of depreciation)	4,000
Total assets	$8,000
Current liabilities	$2,000
Long-term debt (8%)	2,200
Common stock	2,000
Retained earnings	1,800
Total liabilities and net worth	$8,000

Appendix

Table A–1. Future value of a single amount $(1 + r)^n$

Years	*2%*	*4%*	*5%*	*6%*	*8%*	*10%*	*12%*	*14%*	*16%*
1	1.020	1.040	1.050	1.060	1.080	1.100	1.120	1.140	1.160
2	1.040	1.082	1.102	1.124	1.166	1.210	1.254	1.300	1.346
3	1.061	1.124	1.158	1.191	1.260	1.331	1.405	1.482	1.561
4	1.082	1.170	1.216	1.262	1.360	1.464	1.574	1.689	1.811
5	1.104	1.217	1.276	1.338	1.469	1.611	1.762	1.925	2.100
6	1.126	1.265	1.340	1.419	1.587	1.772	1.974	2.195	2.436
7	1.149	1.316	1.407	1.504	1.714	1.949	2.211	2.502	2.826
8	1.172	1.369	1.477	1.594	1.851	2.144	2.476	2.853	3.278
9	1.195	1.423	1.551	1.689	1.999	2.358	2.773	3.252	3.803
10	1.219	1.480	1.629	1.791	2.159	2.594	3.106	3.707	4.411
11	1.243	1.539	1.710	1.898	2.332	2.853	3.479	4.226	5.117
12	1.268	1.601	1.796	2.012	2.518	3.138	3.896	4.818	5.936
13	1.294	1.665	1.886	2.133	2.720	3.452	4.363	5.492	6.886
14	1.319	1.732	1.980	2.261	2.937	3.797	4.887	6.261	7.988
15	1.346	1.801	2.079	2.397	3.172	4.177	5.474	7.138	9.266
20	1.486	2.191	2.653	3.207	4.661	6.727	9.646	13.743	19.461
25	1.641	2.666	3.386	4.292	6.848	10.835	17.000	26.462	40.874
30	1.811	3.243	4.322	5.743	10.063	17.449	29.960	50.950	85.850
40	2.208	4.801	7.040	10.286	21.725	45.259	93.051	188.88	378.72

Table A-2: Present value of a single amount $\frac{1}{(1+r)^n}$

Years	*2%*	*4%*	*5%*	*6%*	*8%*	*10%*	*12%*	*14%*	*16%*
1	0.980	0.962	0.952	0.943	0.926	0.909	0.893	0.877	0.862
2	0.961	0.925	0.907	0.890	0.857	0.826	0.797	0.769	0.743
3	0.942	0.889	0.864	0.840	0.794	0.751	0.712	0.675	0.641
4	0.924	0.855	0.823	0.792	0.735	0.683	0.636	0.592	0.552
5	0.906	0.822	0.784	0.747	0.681	0.621	0.567	0.519	0.476
6	0.888	0.790	0.746	0.705	0.630	0.564	0.507	0.456	0.410
7	0.871	0.760	0.711	0.665	0.583	0.513	0.452	0.400	0.354
8	0.853	0.731	0.677	0.627	0.540	0.467	0.404	0.351	0.305
9	0.837	0.703	0.645	0.592	0.500	0.424	0.361	0.308	0.263
10	0.820	0.676	0.614	0.558	0.463	0.386	0.322	0.270	0.227
11	0.804	0.650	0.585	0.527	0.429	0.350	0.287	0.237	0.195
12	0.788	0.625	0.557	0.497	0.397	0.319	0.257	0.208	0.168
13	0.773	0.601	0.530	0.469	0.368	0.290	0.229	0.182	0.145
14	0.758	0.577	0.505	0.442	0.340	0.263	0.205	0.160	0.125
15	0.743	0.555	0.481	0.417	0.315	0.239	0.183	0.140	0.108
20	0.673	0.456	0.377	0.312	0.215	0.149	0.104	0.073	0.051
25	0.610	0.375	0.295	0.233	0.146	0.092	0.059	0.038	0.024
30	0.552	0.308	0.231	0.174	0.099	0.057	0.033	0.020	0.012
40	0.453	0.208	0.142	0.097	0.046	0.022	0.011	0.005	0.003

Table A-3. Present value of a stream of payments

Years	*2%*	*4%*	*5%*	*6%*	*8%*	*10%*	*12%*	*14%*	*16%*
1	0.980	0.962	0.952	0.943	0.926	0.909	0.893	0.877	0.862
2	1.942	1.886	1.859	1.833	1.783	1.736	1.690	1.647	1.605
3	2.884	2.775	2.723	2.673	2.577	2.487	2.402	2.322	2.246
4	3.808	3.630	3.546	3.465	3.312	3.170	3.037	2.914	2.798
5	4.713	4.452	4.329	4.212	3.993	3.791	3.605	3.433	3.274
6	5.601	5.242	5.076	4.917	4.623	4.355	4.111	3.889	3.685
7	6.472	6.002	5.786	5.582	5.206	4.868	4.564	4.288	4.039
8	7.325	6.733	6.463	6.210	5.747	5.335	4.968	4.639	4.344
9	8.162	7.435	7.108	6.802	6.247	5.759	5.328	4.946	4.607
10	8.983	8.111	7.722	7.360	6.710	6.145	5.650	5.216	4.833
11	9.787	8.760	8.306	7.887	7.139	6.495	5.938	5.453	5.029
12	10.575	9.385	8.863	8.384	7.536	6.814	6.194	5.660	5.197
13	11.384	9.986	9.394	8.853	7.904	7.103	6.424	5.842	5.342
14	12.106	10.563	9.899	9.295	8.244	7.367	6.628	6.002	5.468
15	12.849	11.118	10.380	9.712	8.559	7.606	6.811	6.142	5.575
20	16.351	13.590	12.462	11.470	9.818	8.514	7.469	6.623	5.929
25	19.523	15.622	14.094	12.783	10.675	9.077	7.843	6.873	6.097
30	22.396	17.292	15.372	13.765	11.258	9.427	8.055	7.003	6.177
40	27.355	19.793	17.159	15.046	11.925	9.779	8.244	7.105	6.234

Index